In Her Element

**SEA SALT, SURRENDER, AND A
JOURNEY TO A WHOLE LIFE**

In Her Element

SEA SALT, SURRENDER, AND A JOURNEY TO A WHOLE LIFE

Selina Delangre

For more information, please write:
Best Seller Publishing®
253 N. San Gabriel Blvd, Unit B
Pasadena, CA 91107
or call 1 (626) 765-9750
Visit us online at: www.BestSellerPublishing.org

ENDORSEMENT

*Selina is a gift. With God at her back, coura-
geous vision, and trailblazing perseverance,
Selina has gifted humanity with unprocessed
mineral sea salt, a "natural resource that offers
such a profound impact on our well-being."
Through answers found only from surrender and
in silence, Selina is fulfilling the mission begun
by her inspiring father-in-law, Jacques Delangre.
Meeting Jacques, now almost 40 years ago, and
collaborating with Selina for 25-plus years continue to reveal how to enhance our electrical
and light bodies, our illumination, with magic,
with the alchemy of minerals.*

—Lynne August, M.D.

CONTENTS

CONTENTS

INTRODUCTION

*Some of the most beautiful chapters in our
lives won't have a title until much later.*

—Bob Goff

I WAS 19 when I first met Jacques Delangre, the founder of Celtic Sea Salt® and my future father-in-law. Jacques explained to me that the ocean is composed of sodium, chloride, magnesium, potassium, and calcium, which is the same makeup as the salt that comes from it. But what took my breath away was when Jacques told me that the plasma in our body has the very same composition. It then made complete sense that our bodies would need sea salt rather than table salt. And in this book, I'll explain the difference.

What I have since learned is that the elements of our lives work similarly because everyone has a place in the whole person we have been created to be. Each one plays a role.

We need them all to make us whole, just like the composition of elements in sea salt makes it a whole food.

Salt is an essential ingredient for maintaining a fluid balance in our bodies. It is also an important resource used every day in many aspects of our lives, from manufacturing to water purification and so on.

In a similar way, some elements of our overall lives have a strong impact, and some have a lighter one. I have found that writing about the profound outcomes of some of the decisions I have made has required humility. In other words, I had a really hard time writing about some of the experiences I include in this book. But it is all worth it to me if I can bring a perspective that can be of comfort to someone else.

CONTINUING JACQUES' MISSION

Jacques would often say, "We are having a love affair with sea salt." The love comes from the appreciation of what life would be without it. I am now honored to have this opportunity to share Jacques' message about salt and continue his mission "to source a mineral sea salt that complements our lives." I am also excited to share the stories of how I have survived, even occasionally thrived, as I've continued to explore this natural resource that offers such a profound impact on our well-being.

From the beginning, continuing Jacques' efforts to educate people about sea salt was my intention behind the book—not only with our customers in mind but also for anybody interested in understanding more about the sea salt business.

With the business, I felt it was my responsibility to invest in additional analysis of all our salts for those educating others on the proper nutrients to consume for optimal health. So, from working closely with our chemist, I now understand how to compare salts from a scientific perspective. And through the relationships I've built with global health advocates, I know what they consider a whole, healthy salt to be. I then do the research and due diligence to deliver a trustworthy salt sourced with higher-than-normal standards.

It is likewise as important to analyze the elements that make up a whole life. It's these elements that make us who we are, such as being a mother, a boss, a business owner, a daughter, or a sister—whatever elements you are composed of are filled with experiences and characters that create the composition of your whole existence. While the more challenging experiences, or the stronger elements of life, are really designed to help us grow, whether they are large or small, all these elements are equally important to one another. We have to recognize that in order to find emotional balance and have a life that is whole and authentic.

Eating sodium chloride (refined salt) alone without its complementing elements can cause issues in the body. However, eating unrefined salt with sulfur, magnesium, calcium, potassium, phosphorus, and all the trace elements makes salt beneficial. Similarly, eating sodium with potassium and all the other naturally occurring elements makes salt beneficial. I'll explain more about this in the book, but it works this way, too, with the elements of our lives.

MY LIFE ELEMENTS

> *The Chemist who can extract from his heart's elements compassion, respect, longing, patience, regret, surprise, and forgiveness and compound them into one can create that atom which is called love.*

> —Kahlil Gibran

None of these elements of my life came together by chance. I really believe all of them were divinely orchestrated in the universe, from the way I met my husband to the first salt source I found outside Brittany, France. This book will tell the story of how Jacques Delangre started the Celtic Sea Salt brand and will share some of the health secrets Jacques wrote about in his book *Seasalt's Hidden Powers*. It will touch upon the multiple hurdles the company overcame before and after I came to run it and eventually create Selina Naturally®, as the company is now known.

In the book, I will detail certain challenges I've encountered, such as the fierce competition of what I call the "salty wars" and a brand infringement so bold that the Celtic Sea Salt name was almost taken from us. Every decade, it felt like I was starting a whole new business with the growing

pains of scale-up needs and with keeping up with the industry trends and methods of distribution.

And then there was my personal life: learning how to be
the mother of a special needs child who grew into an adult,
surviving a devastating flood, and coping with the kidnapping and murder of my mentor. My intention with this book is
to show how all these different experiences created the elements that make me who I am today. These elements have
caused me to learn about the power of intention through
the art of putting my attention on what I want instead of
what I don't want. This is still a daily exercise that I have yet
to master.

MY PURPOSE

In all the adversity that I have experienced, what got me
through these tough times is what I think all humans crave:
empathy, or the understanding that someone can relate to
what you are going through. To read or hear about somebody who went through something similar can help us realize that the answers for how to get through adversity are
within us. Once we've tapped into that vibration of related-
ness, we can open up enough to listen and surrender. This is
what I hope this book helps you do.

I want to share with you how I turned feeling out of control and like a victim into being victorious through the teachings of a multitude of future thinkers who have studied the
science of the mind and have spoken about living in creation

versus living in survival. These teachings have impacted my life by inspiring me to work on myself and strengthen my weaknesses.

I also want to offer you what I've learned from my own experience running the company. I learned everything completely hands-on and without any kind of business degree. Every time I realized that I didn't know something, my sister, my staff, my daughters, and I would just go figure it out—all the way from the very beginning with cash flow up until recently with the small business loan programs resulting from the COVID-19 pandemic. Thank God for my niece Stephanie and my sister Teece, who helped in this learning process!

I've watched the company grow from a mail-order operation selling one pound of salt at a time to a company that moves 613 tons of salt each year. What started as a two-person company run out of Jacques and Yvette's house is now a company with 34 employees in an 18,000-square-foot warehouse. Over 40,000 stores carry our products in more than 25 different countries. We also have 2,000 doctors in our database who recommend our salt to their patients.

We have so many testimonials from people who had great results with their health by switching to Celtic Sea Salt (CSS). One customer said her husband hadn't been out of bed for weeks, and after putting a pinch of CSS on his tongue, he started walking around the block. Even I had a hard time believing some of these testimonials, but when you think of sea salt being like a battery charger of electrolytes, it makes sense.

As of 2021, the Celtic Sea Salt brand still comes up as the most-searched sea salt brand on the internet globally. We have paid very few influencers to get these results—this has happened organically, simply from people all over the world sharing the benefits of Celtic Sea Salt. Just go to YouTube and type in "Celtic Sea Salt" and you'll be amazed how many people are talking about it.

In the last 40 years, I've seen the different trends and friction points. I've experienced the challenges of running a sea salt business, from all the legal issues to the research to the sourcing required to bring these salts from all over the world to the marketplace. I've watched the natural products industry grow from a few little health food markets to mass distribution all over the world, and I've learned what a big responsibility it is to take a commodity, import it, and re-distribute it all over the world as a food item.

LEARNING TO LIVE IN CREATION

My experience raising a special needs child is another element of my life. I gave birth to Dominic when I was only 20, and he lived to be 28 years old with some fairly extreme issues caused by his cerebral palsy and seizures. I'm sharing this experience with the hope it could be a support to you or someone you know but also because I want to keep Dominic real.

I find myself forgetting what my life was like when he was still here in the physical, even though he was such a part of what has made me who I am today. He taught me empathy, compassion, unconditional love, humility, courage, and an understanding of what it means to "just be." Dominic did all this, even though he never spoke a word.

Between the business and my family, every day was like a whitewater rafting trip, just trying to figure out how to get to the end with everyone as safe as possible. I wouldn't have gotten through it without the help and support of my family and friends and the spiritual leaders who shared their knowledge and stories through their books. God always knew what book I needed, and it would almost fall off the shelf so I could be empowered by the teachings.

Recently, I read Joe Dispenza's *Breaking the Habit of Being Yourself*, which focuses on living in creation versus living in survival mode, or autopilot. When we focus on an unwanted past or a dreaded future, this is when we live in stress or survival mode. This is where I was for 30 years! So, as I relived these experiences through writing the book, it brought up some deep emotions at times. There were things I didn't realize I still needed to forgive myself for. And I realized that I eventually got through, not by trying to fix my circumstances but by surrendering to them and waiting for solutions to come to me.

I also plan to share the spiritual journey I went through. I was born and raised Catholic, then became born-again Christian, and now my relationship with God is through my prayers and meditation. I am closer to God's influence than I have ever been, and I feel that I have become almost an expert at surrendering. I now know that even in the future, like in the past, I will come up against things and I won't know what the heck to do. But it's in surrendering, or letting go and letting God lead, and asking the right questions that I will meet and overcome my obstacles. It takes silence to hear the answers.

I have experienced so many mixed emotions in writing my stories down for you, even fear that you might read this and have an unkind opinion of my truth. But I've come to the realization that this is another surrender experience. The opportunity has presented itself to write this book, and I have surrendered to doing it. I will push through these fears just the way I have so many others.

In his recent book *Greenlights*, Matthew McConaughey calls experiences like this "green lights." More challenging experiences, he says, are like red or yellow lights that eventually turn green.

INTENDED AUDIENCE

This book should appeal to the entrepreneur spirit in general and to that person who has something inside of them that they want to do but are afraid to try. It should also appeal to anyone with a special needs child, because while that won't be the focus, it is a significant part of my journey. Most of all, I hope that reading this book inspires you to do something you've dreamed of. Because I'm telling you, if I can do it, anybody can.

So, I encourage you to dive in and read my story. I hope that from it you will better understand the importance of minerals and eating whole foods, especially whole sea salt. I hope this book will even help you to "make friends with sea salt," as Jacques would say, and to better appreciate the origins and sources that make it such a God-created blessing. It is my intention for you to be inspired by my experiences, the way I have been inspired by so many stories I have read. We all have our own stories. It's what makes us whole. This has been such a blessing to be able to share mine and all the gratitude I have for what makes us who we are.

1

Finding My Element: An Introduction to Sea Salt

Finding your element is about realizing what you love and are good at. God and the Universe will continue presenting opportunities that will be stepping stones to you finding your element, even though you might not recognize them as such when they appear.

WHEN I LEFT Muncie, Indiana, for Chico, California, at the age of 19, I had no clue that one day I would be in the sea salt business. I'd never even heard of "sea" salt. It was the late '70s, and nobody around me talked about health food or any health products like they do today.

This move came about because I decided I needed to go to college because that's what you do when you grow up. My mom couldn't afford to pay for it, but I heard through the grapevine (not through the internet because there was no internet then) that you could get residency status in California after living there for a full year. Then I could attend college, paying only in-state tuition, which was more affordable. So, I picked a place on a whim: Chico, a small college town a couple of hours north of Sacramento.

I took a bus from Muncie to Chico with Cindy, a high school friend of my sister Teece. I had worked several jobs to save enough money to move, get an apartment, and pay for a footlocker full of junk food like ramen noodles to survive on until we got jobs. I had relatives I'd visited in Southern California, but no friends or relatives this far north, so we were on our own. I had no fear, only imagination, insatiable curiosity, and the belief that there wasn't anything I couldn't get through. At the age of 19, we all think we are invincible.

After Cindy and I arrived in Chico and found an apartment, the first thing we did was walk down to the Goodwill, about four blocks away, to pick out a couch and a coffee table. As we were carrying the furniture to our apartment, this hippie guy stopped in a big green flatbed truck. He had a beard and a black and white dog in the front seat. "You need a hand?" And we said, "Sure, we would love one!"

We loaded the couch onto his truck, and he even helped us get it up the stairs to the small one-bedroom apartment on the second floor. As he was leaving, he gave me his business card. "I'm Philippe. Call me if you ever need anything." The only thing in the apartment was a bulletin board, so I took his business card and stuck it there. I then told Cindy that it would be a great story to tell my grandchildren: how I met their grandfather. Somehow, I just knew, because lo and behold, he was my future husband.

What were the chances of that happening, of me and my friend walking down the street at exactly the time he was driving down it? But it happened, and Philippe and I began dating. Soon enough, he wanted to introduce me to his parents, Jacques and Yvette, who lived about 45 minutes from Chico in the town of Paradise.

WHAT IS SEA SALT?

Sodium is sodium, and chloride is chloride. These elements in table salt and sea salt are not different from each other. The part that makes sea salt beneficial and not harmful is the other naturally occurring elements within sea salt, such as magnesium, potassium, and calcium. These other elements allow the sodium and chloride to communicate properly in the body in how to assimilate these elements.

—Jacques Delangre

*Lunch with (right to left) Yvette, Jacques,
and Cynthia, my sister-in-law*

My introduction to Philippe's parents was surreal for a 19-year-old Midwestern girl raised on a typical American diet. I really did not have a clue that food played any role in our health or well-being, and when walking into Jacques and Yvette's house for the first time, everything smelled completely unfamiliar: brown rice cooking and fresh-baked bread. It was just such a great smell and made my mouth instantly water. I remember Yvette was at the stove, and Jacques came walking into the kitchen with a big, beautiful smile and said, "Hello, my name is Jacques." We shook hands.

A little later, Philippe's sister Cynthia joined us, and we all sat down to lunch.

They asked if I knew anything about macrobiotics. I had never heard of them. They explained to me that it's a lifestyle and a way of eating. I was very intrigued.

Ever since puberty, I had suffered these bad migraine headaches that the doctors and my mother never had any answers for. Some days, I lived off headache medicine, just so that I could function. So, when they started to talk about the foods that we were eating and the macrobiotic lifestyle, there was something inside of me that said, "That makes so much sense. Gosh, no wonder I have such bad migraine headaches."

I received the information that they were sharing with me at the table without any skepticism. And when I took some brown rice on my plate, they said, "Would you like some gomasio on your brown rice?"

I asked, "What is that?"

They said, "Well, it's fresh-roasted sesame seeds ground with sea salt."

"Sea salt?" I asked. "What is sea salt?"

Now, over 40 years later, I can easily answer that question with the help of Jacques' book *Seasalt's Hidden Powers*, which he gave me at the time. In the next section, I'm going to walk you through some of the points about what makes sea salt so remarkable.

THE IMPORTANCE OF OLIGO ELEMENTS
(MACRO VS. MICRO)

Seasalt's Hidden Powers relates the research that Jacques undertook by talking to salt experts around the world. He spoke seven different languages, so his research was extensive. He was able to communicate with people through phone calls and letters (remember there was no internet in the '70s) about their research on sea salt and minerals, how important they are, and the bioavailability of them in our body. This was the beginning of what my daughter Colette coined as "changing the reputation of salt." Today, most people have at least heard of sea salt. Maybe you've even heard that it's supposed to be better for you than "regular" salt.

The question I often get is, how many minerals are in Celtic Sea Salt? People are then surprised by the answer to the question of *how much* of each mineral it contains, since they seem like such small amounts. The best way to explain this is that nature has created a whole salt with the elements divinely proportioned at the micro level to mirror our own plasma composition.

The main idea here is that the body needs certain minerals, which we call "essential minerals." Essential minerals are sometimes divided into two categories: major minerals (macro-minerals) and trace minerals (microminerals). These two groups of minerals are equally important, but trace minerals are needed in smaller amounts than major minerals. Note that the amounts needed in the body are not an indication of their importance.

The role of trace minerals in human nutrition is well recognized by public health agencies, nutritionists, and researchers from various areas of knowledge. Although they represent a barely quantifiable part of the human constitution, they are essential for our metabolic balance. They are the catalysts of our biological functions. A lack, or an insufficient amount, of a nutrient can result in a deficiency disease, which can be life-threatening in extreme cases.

Oligos in Greek means "a very tiny quantity," so oligo elements, or trace elements, are pure trace minerals that are present in the organism in minute quantities. They are necessary for the development of animal and vegetable life. Although they represent a barely quantifiable part of the human constitution, they are essential for our metabolic balance.

Oligotherapy is widely recognized throughout Europe as a powerful treatment for bacterial infections, cardiovascular disease, respiratory infections, circulatory disorders, and neurological conditions. Oligotherapy uses oligo elements to normalize enzyme and hormonal functions to regulate the homeostasis of the body. This form of therapy provides the body with the ions that it cannot synthesize and that are indispensable for cellular enzymatic functions. It uses highly bioavailable forms of trace elements in small, precisely measured doses.

Sea salt offers oligo elements, but "regular," or table, salt does not, and the main reason for that is in how it is processed. I will come back to this later in the chapter.

SEA SALT'S HIDDEN POWERS

Now, I have thousands and thousands of customers who have had their own positive experiences using Celtic Sea Salt, including some who even call me and say their blood pressure has gone down since they've been eating it. So, I have other people's testimonials to really confirm Jacques' claims.

All the points that follow are from Jacques' book. I'm not just making them up. You can also do a Google search for "benefits of eating salt," and you will see that salt plays a role in every organ in the body. It's a scientific truth that our body needs the elements sodium (salt) and chloride. Now, again, by "salt," I do not mean table salt.

I'm talking about sea salt. The question "How many minerals are in your salt?" comes up a lot. The number has been estimated at 84, 72, and so on. When someone asks me this question, I like to answer, "All of them" and tell them that I have lost count. All the minerals are present in seawater, and they impart way into the sea salt. In truth, we test for 72 elements. Some results show a "less than" value to a certain percentage. This shows how sensitive the test is. If the test result is "less than," then it is not measured with that sensitivity. So, I do not like to say specifically how many minerals are in the salt. I think it's reasonable to say that the salt contains about 60 minerals and trace minerals. This is why unrefined sea salt is a much better choice than ordinary table salt bought at the supermarket. Table salt has been stripped of its companion elements and contains additives to keep it powdery so it can pour well, which I'll talk more about in the next section.

The only thing a table salt user might miss is that while sea salt contains some naturally occurring iodine, there's not enough to meet your daily recommended amount. That's why we recommend eating seaweed, which is high in iodine, and also why we created our Celtic Seaweed Seasoning, which has over 260 micrograms (mcg) of iodine per serving.

In the following, I will elaborate on some of the health benefits that Jacques Delangre wrote about in his book *Seasalt's Hidden Powers.* He says:

- *Salt is most effective in stabilizing an irregular heart-beat. And contrary to the misconception that it causes high blood pressure, it is essential for the regulation of blood pressure—in conjunction with the water. Naturally, the proportions are critical.* Because of the sodium and the chloride being balanced and supported with magnesium, potassium, and calcium, sea salt is supportive of body functions.
- *Salt is vital to the extraction of excess acidity from the cells in the body, particularly the brain cells.* Table salt is more acidic. Celtic Sea Salt is more alkaline, and with an alkaline environment your body can better fight off disease. It can help particularly with brain cells. Your brain really has to have an alkaline environment to be able to function optimally.
- *Salt is vital for balancing the sugar levels in the blood and a needed element for diabetics.* It's really the bio-

available minerals like potassium that help support
the conditions that a diabetic might have. There's a
potassium pump in our body that opens and closes.
When it opens, it lets the sodium in; when it closes, it
lets the potassium out. You must have the molecules
of sodium and potassium together for the potassium
pump to even work. Diabetics have a potassium deficiency and are supposed to take extra potassium.
You can do a Google search for an image of a sodium
potassium pump to see how it works.

- *Salt is vital for the generation of the hydroelectric
  energy in the cells and the body. It is used for local power
  generation at the sites of the energy that is needed by
  the cells.* Basically, if you were to put sea salt in a glass
  of water and then put a magnet and a light bulb in the
  glass, you could make the light bulb light up. You can
  see this experiment on YouTube. This is what sea salt
  does for our body. It makes energy in the cells.

- *Salt is vital for the communication information process
  in the nervous system, and it works from the moment of
  conception to death.* Sea salt is a combination of over
  60 different minerals, which function as electrolytes
  or electrical connectors. Each one of these combined
  elements plays an important role with one another so
  that they might have negative effects by themselves
  but together they support the body.

- *Salt is vital for the absorption of food particles through
  the intestinal tract.* If you put a little pinch of salt on

your tongue, it activates your digestive system. This is because sea salt promotes hydrochloric acid, which initiates the digestive system in the mouth.

- *Salt is vital for clearance of the lungs of mucus plugs and sticky phlegm, particularly in asthma and cystic fibrosis.* If you gargle with this salt or do nasal washes with a neti pot, it helps to get rid of congestion and any asthma problems.
- *Salt is vital for clearing congestion in the sinuses and is a strong, natural antihistamine.* Just like an inhaler for asthma, if you go into a salt room, it helps the lungs open and expand more.
- *Salt is essential for the prevention of muscle cramps.* Athletes will drink Gatorade because of all the different minerals in it. But if you just put some sea salt in water with lemon, you have the same thing, and with no sugar.
- *Salt is vital for making the structure of the bones firm. Osteoporosis, in a major way, is the result of a salt and water shortage in the body.* Our bones are about 20 percent water, and that water is a very salty solution of magnesium, potassium, sodium, and other minerals and elements. If you are deficient in them, your bones will get very brittle. Irma Jennings, a holistic bone coach, posed the question "Do your bones need salt?" on her blog. In this post, she wrote about a study conducted by the Women's Health Initiative a few years back that showed sodium intake may not

impact osteoporosis in postmenopausal women as once suspected. In fact, lower levels of sodium intake seemed to have little effect on fractures and bone mineral density, while increased sodium intake resulted in stronger bones, higher bone mineral density, and fewer hip fractures over the six years the study covered. Fereydoon Batmanghelidj's book *Water: Rx for a Healthier, Pain-Free Life* also covered some of this information about osteoporosis that Jacques included in his book. He was one of the doctors who confirmed that Jacques was on the right track. He was also one of our amazing influencers who really gave our salts recognition out there in the world. I'll talk more about the influencers in the next chapter.

- *Salt on the tongue will stop a persistent, dry cough.* One of our influencers, Tess Master, is a voice-over actress in California. When she starts to get a dry mouth or a cough that she can't control, she just puts a pinch of our Celtic Sea Salt on her tongue.
- *Salt is vital for prevention of gout and gouty arthritis.* As I've said, it's really about the minerals. When your body has any mineral deficiencies, symptoms like these can occur.
- *Salt is vital for maintaining sexuality and libido.* When you have mineral deficiencies, it can throw your hormones off balance.
- *Salt is vital for the prevention of varicose veins and spider veins on the legs and thighs.* Again, if your body has

the optimal supply of minerals, then it doesn't have these issues.

And now, since the coronavirus pandemic in 2020, the natural products industry is skyrocketing because you need a strong immune system to fight off illness. People are even more interested in making healthy choices, and the bottom line is that sea salt is healthier than table salt. To really understand the difference, think of it like eating whole foods with all the nutrients still intact versus foods that have been stripped of nutrients through processing. To get a better idea of how this might work, let's look at how both types of salt are processed.

HOW SALT IS PROCESSED (TABLE VS. SEA SALT)

There are many different types of salts: potassium salts, magnesium salts, and so on. Table salt is 99 percent sodium chloride, with a pH of seven. Since sea salt also includes minerals, the sodium chloride content varies anywhere between 79 and 89 percent, with a pH of eight to ten. This is why sea salt enhances the flavor of food instead of overpowering it and also why you see the growing trend of chefs now using sea salt.

Both sodium and chloride ions have important functions. Sodium regulates blood pressure and plays a role in transmitting messages between nerves and muscles. Chloride is a component of hydrochloric acid needed for digestion.

The job of maintaining the right concentration of minerals in the blood falls to the kidneys. If the levels of sodium chloride in the blood rise from the ingestion of too much salt, the kidneys will excrete less water to dilute the blood and maintain the proper salt concentration. This, however, has the effect of increasing blood volume, which can lead to increased blood pressure and swelling in tissues as water leaks out of the bloodstream.

Thirst often accompanies a large intake of salt because water will also be drawn out of cells to help maintain the right concentration of salt in the bloodstream.

Over the years, we've taken whole foods and tried to make them more convenient for the consumer. But rarely does anyone ask, "What effect might making this more convenient for the kitchen have on the body?"

In contrast to the production of table salt, which I'll get to next, the traditional way of making salt takes a lot more time. It really depends on the region, but in Brittany—one of the regions we have sourced from since the beginning—it takes *seven years* for each salt pond to gain that perfect harmonious balance of magnesium, potassium, calcium, and all the other elements of a good sea salt. So, you can really appreciate the slow process.

Then it could take seven weeks for the saltwater to crystallize. In addition, the salt is only able to be produced in the warmer months, from May to about September. And as a seasonal commodity, you have a limited supply. A scale-up certainly does not happen overnight.

Now, if you go to the Morton Salt website, you can see the company is very proud of the research it did to find out how to provide the consumer with a salt that reliably flows out of a container without caking. The company had its eye on innovation, and it did a good thing in that respect. It's more convenient. You don't have to pound the salt to get it out of a container like you do when salt doesn't have the free-flowing agents added. Sea salt can become hard and form clumps because it attracts moisture.

But just because it's convenient doesn't mean it's the best complement that our body should have. This is because to create a salt that pours perfectly, Morton had to add special agents. And since the free-flowing agents cause the salt to have a different flavor, they had to add some dextrose, or sugar, to make the flavor a little bit better. So, when you see "pure" table salt, it actually has additives to make it pour so easily. I could go into all the details about the centrifuge and the separators and everything, but what I really want to get across is that, just like with any food, processing salt makes it void of other essential elements.

Over the years, I have traveled all over the world looking at different ways salt is harvested. Later in the book, I will share with you some of the different variations, but at the end of the day, the basic differences between table salt and our salt are in the minerals and the processing. It just makes sense that we really should be eating foods that have all their original nutrients. You can see an in-depth mineral analysis for each of the salts in our CSS line.

LIKE POETRY

> *Blood can also be thought of as a private ocean, a recapitulation of what life was like for all the years we spent drifting as microscopic, single-celled organisms, taking up nutrients from seawater and then eliminating waste products back into seawater. Not only is blood mostly water but the watery portion of blood, the plasma, has a concentration of salt and other ions that is remarkably similar to seawater.*

> —Andrew Schafer, MD
> Professor of Medicine in Hematology-
> Oncology at Weill Cornell Medical College

While I don't remember Jacques' exact words when he first explained to me sea salt those 40-some years ago, it went something like the quote above. It was as if he were speaking poetry. The words just flowed from his mouth like a natural-born teacher. He explained that our bodies are made up of 70 percent water, and the ocean is made up of 70 percent water. The ocean has sodium, magnesium, calcium, potassium, and chloride, and our bodies have magnesium, potassium, sodium chloride, and calcium.

I just kept listening, thinking, "Why was I not taught that in science class?" If I was, I had not been paying any attention, because as I sat there at that table it gave me goose bumps. It just made so much sense that our bodies were supposed to eat the salt that has the same mineral composition as, or one very similar to, sea salt. But it was intuition, not science, saying to me, "That makes sense. I don't ever want to eat anything else other than whole foods again."

This is how the Delangres got me. It wasn't a cult or anything, even though I think my family thought it was at the beginning. That's how completely I changed my entire lifestyle.

I remember going back to my little apartment and opening my footlocker. I was hungry, but I just looked at all that junk food and said, "Ooh, I can't eat any of that." It had been such an eye-opening experience for me. At that time, I didn't really have a clear plan for my future, but now that I look back, I can see this was just a little stepping stone, another experience in one element in my life preparing me for where I was going next.

At first, it was exciting to find a lifestyle that could help me get rid of my migraine headaches. I got into eating healthy, and I felt so much better. But soon I would discover that in life there are no perfect solutions. I also understood that anything that made the slightest difference in how I felt was a change worth embracing.

When I got pregnant for the first time, I had so much cocky confidence that I was going to have the most perfect, healthy baby as a result of my diet. The humbling was about to begin because anyone can experience challenges, even when following clean eating practices. In my case, Dominic was born with special needs for reasons that likely had nothing to do with what I did or didn't eat. Of course, a proper nutritious diet provides the best foundation for a healthy baby, but the Universe had something else in mind for my journey with Dominic. I'll get to this part of my story soon enough.

I now understand that we have all come here to explore how to support all the elements of our lives to be the best according to our abilities. It is different for everyone. When I look back, it seems that it was all laid out exactly the way it was supposed to be. Why did I meet Jacques? Why did I get into this business? Why did I have a special needs child? These characters and experiences are elements of my life that were intended to all come together.

In the next chapter, I'll tell Jacques and Yvette's story of how the Celtic Sea Salt brand came to be.

2

The Sea Salt Revolution: Jacques' Mission to Reveal Seasalt's Hidden Powers

It is not the strongest of the species that survives, nor the most intelligent. It is the one that is most adaptable to change.

—Charles Darwin

BEFORE JACQUES DELANGRE started the whole sea salt revolution globally, the term "sea salt" wasn't really in use unless you were talking about something directly related to the ocean. It was not an option at the grocery store or something that you might expect to find at the table. At that time, there was just table salt.

Jacques was born in 1925 in New Jersey to Belgian parents, who then returned with him to Belgium, where he was raised. He didn't return to the United States until 1947, after he met Yvette in Paris and they were married. In France, they had consumed a very typical French diet, and they started to have some real health problems. Yvette was diagnosed with cancer in her ovaries, and Jacques' issue was that he would sometimes just pass out. He would be sitting at a table, and, for no explicable reason, he would fall over.

Doctors didn't know what to do for Jacques since they didn't know what was wrong with him. Yvette had already had her three children at this point, and the doctors wanted to remove her uterus. Since she decided to not have the surgery and no one knew what to do for Jacques, they started on their own journey to understand the body and to discover how they could have optimal health and well-being. This was what led them to macrobiotics.

Keep in mind that it wasn't like today, when you can just type "I keep passing out" and then good old Google tells you what to do. Back then, there were few people looking at health and nutrition or the body's well-being. It was mainly medical doctors recommending surgery or prescribing medication.

Nutrition was a high priority for the Delangres, so they educated themselves on natural living and holistic healing. Most people still did not fully understand the contribution that different foods made to your body, good or bad, or what problems certain deficiencies caused. So, once Jacques and Yvette started to understand more about this, they came to see that sea salt was essential for the body's well-being.

While he was educating himself about sea salt, Jacques also developed an extensive knowledge of Do-In, the ancient art of self-diagnosis and therapeutic massage. Both through his own studies and the teachings of Japanese scholar Michio Kushi, Jacques was inspired to write *The First Book of Do-In*. This book was published for the first time in 1971, in a dual-language English and French edition. It has since been published in German, Italian, Spanish, and Portuguese. The book really skyrocketed in Portugal and Brazil, where this was a big movement. Jacques also created a meridian chart that people used in acupuncture and acupressure. He told people how important it was to keep your meridians massaged and stimulated.

Also of note was Jacques' passion for self-leavened whole wheat bread. He worked with relatives in their Belgian *boulangerie* (bakery), and in time Jacques developed his own recipes. His delectable loaves were made from the finest Montana whole grain wheat, which he milled fresh in his stone mill. The bread was seasoned with natural unrefined Celtic Sea Salt, leavened by the dough's own naturally occurring yeast (sourdough), and then baked in his wood-fired brick oven. The result was the most beautiful loaves, exuding a wonderful, hardy bread aroma and a taste that would complement any gourmet meal. He taught many classes in bread baking and helped start several bakeries across the United States, one of which is French Meadow Bakery, founded by Lynn Gordon.

Both Jacques and Yvette shared what they had learned by teaching natural health philosophy through lectures, cooking classes, and study groups. Jacques was also invited to lecture throughout the United States, France, Belgium, England, and Italy.

Jacques was educating people on sea salt even before he came to write *Seasalt's Hidden Powers* in 1979, or the booklet that came before it. He was influenced to write about sea salt by George Ohsawa, a macrobiotic master in Belgium. They'd both read René Quinton's book, *L'eau de Mer, Milieu Organique,* which established scientifically the relationship between seawater and blood plasma. Quinton's book also explained how important it is to have minerals in a whole form, such as sea salt, which comes from seawater. When he read this, Jacques thought the same thing I did when he explained it all to me: that makes sense.

George Ohsawa urged Jacques to let people know there are differences between salts. He needed to educate the world about it. So, Jacques started to do his own research. Being able to read, write, and speak in seven different languages, he dove into learning about the healing properties of different salts. This reminded him how, growing up years and years ago, one of his French relatives always had a coarse greyish salt on the table. He had paid no real attention to it at the time, but now he wondered how they could find it.

JACQUES' MANTRA: ONLY EAT THE GREY SALT

Soon enough, Jacques tracked this salt he remembered to Brittany, where it was being hand-harvested from salt ponds. The ponds were square, so from an aerial view, they almost looked like rice paddies or fields. They were all lined with a really, *really* thick layer of clay. This clay had a greenish-grey color to it, which gave the salt its recognizable greyish color.

At the time, Jacques speculated that sea salt was nutritious because of its grey color and that white salt lacked nutrition. That's why he started to tell people, "You should only be eating this light grey salt, because if it's light grey, it has all these nutrients in it." Because Jacques was an educator now, people listened to him when he told them how important this salt was for them to eat.

When Jacques first went to Brittany to meet with the president of the salt cooperative in the early '70s, he took a really old video camera because he wanted to capture how the salt was being harvested. (You can go to our "Celtic Sea Salt" YouTube page at **www.youtube.com/celticseasalt** to see his recordings.) On the tour, the president said, "I am curious about you coming here, wanting to educate people on this kind of salt and the history of it, because we have seen a decline in demand."

Because of the lack of demand, the salt cooperative wasn't producing as much salt. Most of the families in the area who had harvested the salt through several generations had moved away because the processed food industry had overtaken their livelihoods. So, they had stopped priming and preparing the region's artisan salt flats to produce salt.

Jacques told the president that he had been teaching people about the virtues of this grey salt and that demand would soon be increasing. "We'll need more salt," he said.

The president said, "That's not something that can happen overnight."

These are the ponds that I mentioned in the previous chapter. Each pond would take seven years to become perfectly balanced with the right pH and saline solution and for the right flora to develop. But once the salt ponds were balanced, they could produce a new harvest every year.

So, on his first few visits, Jacques would just bring some salt back with him in his suitcase. He did this for a few years.

THE GRAIN & SALT SOCIETY MEMBERSHIP

Sure enough, as Jacques educated more people about the salt, more people started wanting it. Shortly before he published his first salt booklet, Jacques had some people over at his house and one guy said, "Can I take some of that salt home?" Jacques said, "Sure."

"Well, how much is it?" Jacques was generous, so he said, "How much do you have in your pocket?" And the guy said, "I have a $5 bill." Jacques said, "Okay, $5 a pound. One pound is yours." And that's how the price of the Celtic Sea Salt was set.

So, when Jacques completed his first version of *Seasalt's Hidden Powers*, a little booklet of about 12 pages, he included details for purchasing salt in the back. The booklet included the composition of sea salt, the composition of our blood plasma, and the way table salt is processed, and then at the back of the book, it said that for $5, you could get a pound of sea salt at The Grain & Salt Society.

He called the society this because in macrobiotics, about 75 percent of your diet is grains. He started a membership as well, since supply was an issue. It was $15 a year to be a member, and the main perk was that in the case of high demand, members would get the salt first. That's how the membership started, and with it the sea salt movement.

In 1976, Jacques officially started importing the grey salt from Brittany with his first purchase order of one 22-pound bag. Soon enough, news of the salt got out to people beyond his little circle. It was the late '70s, and more people were on health journeys. They had already tapped into other pioneers in this revolution of "You are what you eat." So, people would pass his booklet around or take it to the professional advisors they were going to for other health-conscious education.

Jacques published the book version of *Seasalt's Hidden Powers* in 1979, but it was due to the influencers that this whole thing exploded. One of these people was Bruce West. He has a newsletter called *Health Alert*. Others included William Campbell Douglass, MD; Julian Whitaker, MD; Christiane Northrup, MD; David "Avocado" Wolfe; Sally

Fallon, founder of the Weston A. Price Foundation; and Lynne August, MD, who has recently just developed a new electrolyte liquid to complement the minerals of the Celtic Sea Salt.

Each of these professionals had their patients and others who followed their advice through their wellness newsletters and their books. They didn't have the speed of social media to reach people, but their influence was still just as powerful. They would say to people, "Have you heard about this sea salt?" Then they'd give them Jacques' book.

William Campbell Douglass, in particular, had over 80,000 subscribers to his newsletter. In it, he wrote (this is the actual paragraph): "Our bodies need whole foods, whole rice, whole sugar, whole salt. The only salt you should eat is the salt that's grey from The Grain & Salt Society. And you just send those people $5, and they'll send you some salts."

And then boom, overnight the business took off.

Suddenly, Jacques and Yvette were getting all these $5 bills in envelopes at the post office. Not one or two envelopes but big boxes of letters. All these people wanted a pack of the grey salt. Frequently they would have to send the $5 back because of a lack of supply.

It got to be very complicated. Some people said, "No, I don't want the $5 back. Just hang on to it until you have more salt." I have files—old, old files—of all this handwritten correspondence. "Please keep my $5 until you get salt again."

If somebody wanted a five-pound bag of salt, they'd have to say, "I'm sorry, I can only give you one pound of salt right now." Finally, they were able to start making more salt in

Brittany. Today, they still have salt flats producing all the salt we need. So, eventually, we had to reinvent the membership, giving it a value beyond being first in line if we ran out of salt. Running a company is about being able to adapt to changes. And so, we turned that $15 membership into a newsletter. Members also got discounts on other things because supply was not the issue anymore.

Running a company is also about patience in the face of adversity. There have been a lot of roller-coaster rides. I've had friction points and adversities both in my personal life and in running the business. I've learned that it's how well you adapt, and how well you anticipate the future, in my opinion, that is going to be the means of your success.

Over the years, I've kept with me these stories of the sourcing scarcity in the company's beginnings, and in my mental archives there's been something telling me that this one source of sea salt was not sustainable (that it would lead to a lack of supply), and that it was not even scalable. What if something happened to the region? This was something I always had in the back of my mind: you had better go find a salt that compares to this one in another region. If you don't, you won't have a company. That's what I tried to do over the years, which I'll talk more about in upcoming chapters.

I have also remained so thankful that Jacques decided to sell the salt for $5 a pound. Thank you, God, that the guy pulled $5 out of his pocket because with all the adversity and all the things that this company has had to spend money on to survive, if the price had been anything less than $5, we probably couldn't have done it. Today, many of our salts are still close to $5 a pound, and all the other sea salt companies have copied our pricing.

LESSONS

I think the basic lesson here is probably obvious: if you're going to go out there and start a revolution by educating people on your product, you need to have a supply that can meet the demand. That's important. I thought I had that down, I really did. I used this story to motivate me to secure our supplies by researching other salts and just praying to God to bring the other salts from all over the world. So, I made sure I had those supplies.

But with the global pandemic in 2020, our salt was suddenly in greater demand than I'd ever experienced. I had never seen this volume of sea salt being sold.

Even though we have other salts, I'm having a hard time converting people away from the grey one. Jacques' teaching, and our continued teaching as a company, had done such a great job convincing people, "If it's not grey, don't eat it!" People call and say, "I want to order a pallet of your light grey salt." And we say "You know what, we're having a supply issue and we won't have it for about three weeks. We do have this amazing salt from Colima or from Guatemala that has an even better mineral profile. Can we go ahead and sell you a pallet of that?"

Nope. They want to wait for the grey stuff. We have done such a great job that we can't even convert any of our own customers to a salt that we think is just as good! That's really a profound statement of what Jacques started, and how long it has stuck. I am hopeful this book will help give our customers the same confidence in our other salts, since they all have similar, if not better, properties.

FOLLOWING A PATH OF HEALTH AND NUTRITION

Jacques was a visionary, but because of his insatiable curiosity, he was not well respected in his family. I became like him, in this respect, when I decided to follow this path of health and nutrition. Now I'm the one who is blessed, I guess, to continue the sea salt part of Jacques' legacy. It's just a small segment of the impact that Jacques really made on the natural products movement, but thanks to him I now know how essential it is not just to have sea salt in our bodies but also to have the right sea salt.

Today, people are making so much money with health products, but in the '70s Jacques' family thought he was ridiculous. Even his brother often made fun of him. If you remember the days back before bottled water, when companies first started selling it, people laughed. "Who is going to buy a bottle of water?" He faced this same mindset. Who is going to spend $5 for a pound of salt? But as Jacques started to gain more success, his family did start to take him a little more seriously.

There was no real discord with my own family because of my lifestyle choices, but if I walked into the room, it was like, "Oh, here she comes with her philosophy." Also, my choosing to have a child naturally at home instead of in the hospital was not well received.

The irony was that my sisters were both pregnant at about the same time I was, and they didn't even think about health and nutrition, as I explained in the previous chapter. When I would see them eating junk food, I was so arrogant. I would think, "Oh my gosh, what are they doing? This is their baby!" That is how Jacques and Yvette had taught me.

But then I was the one to have a child with special needs, while their children were born completely fine. I went from being so arrogant I thought my poop didn't stink to "Holy crap! I'm going to shut my mouth from now on." In the next chapter, I'll tell the story of how this element of my life came to be.

3

The Salty Wars: Internal and External Battles

*When you change the way you look at
things, the things you look at change.*

—Wayne Dyer

I MAY HAVE been the only person to think of them as the "salty wars," but that's how fierce the competition seemed at times. My maiden name was also Guerra, meaning "war." So, it's kind of a play on my name: Selina Guerra, or salty wars. Like any battle, the salty wars required strategy, such as cultivating relationships with influencers and collaborating with people over new ways of looking at food and lifestyles. While Jacques was busy fighting these salty wars, I was dealing with my own personal struggles.

Jacques had two names for the salt that he used interchangeably when he wrote or talked about it: Celtic Sea Salt and Light Grey Celtic Sea Salt. We have since registered both as trademarks, just to protect that intellectual property. I'll talk about this more in upcoming chapters, but it has not been an easy name to protect.

The wars were not just about protecting the name but also about making sure the grey salt was known and respected over the salt sold by a growing number of competitors. Jacques came up with the name "Celtic Sea Salt" after he first visited Brittany to see how the salt was harvested. While he was there, he discovered a very romantic story about how the Celts had harvested with this method more than 2,000 years ago.

While the name of our salt made sense to Jacques because of the story, it often seems odd to people first discovering it. As I started to get more involved in the company, the first thing people often asked me was, "Did it come from the Celtic Sea?" The water source for our Brittany salt is the Atlantic Ocean.

I explained in the last chapter about how Jacques really tried to educate people on how important it was to eat light grey sea salt. He would also say that it was very important to eat it wet. "Don't let it dry up," he would tell people. "It's lost its minerals if it's dried up."

What gave Jacques credibility to make these kinds of statements was an analysis that he had done by a university in Europe in 1976. This analysis of seawater led Jacques to believe that it matched the results of an analysis of sea salt. However, when he lectured, there was still always somebody in the audience who wanted to argue that their salt was better than his.

I don't know if other food product companies, like in sugar or flour manufacturing, ever had these kinds of wars or the battles trying to prove mine is better than yours. But I do know that in the history of this company this trend has continued. In the health food community especially, there is a lot of fear about putting things that aren't good for you into your body, so people really run with this tactic.

MY HOME BIRTH

While the salty wars were still Jacques' to fight, since he was running the company, I was preparing for my own battle, although I didn't know it yet. The date was January 1, 1979, and we were the stereotypical hippie family living with minimal luxuries. This was at the tail end of the women's rights movement, which was empowering mothers to have home births with a midwife rather than at a hospital with a doctor, who was usually male, in control of the whole birth process. I was 20 years old and getting ready to give birth in the new travel trailer where Philippe and I lived, parked on my sister-in-law's property in Paradise, California. In the surrounding community of somewhat rural Northern California, the practice of home birth was so common that it seemed more normal to have one than not. Plenty of women did so successfully.

My mom and my grandma had come from Indiana to be there with me. When I tell this story, I can't imagine how my mom handled this choice of mine so fearlessly, and with grace, since she'd had all her children in the hospital. But my grandma had all but one of her five at home. My in-laws were going to act as midwives since they had helped with their other grandchildren, and those births had all turned out great.

After listening to Philippe's sister Cynthia talk about her experience, I really had no fear. The labor started just like normal, or so I thought. But I had no clue what a typical birth was like, or what the indicators were that it wasn't going smoothly. And while in labor, the whole process felt blurred and vague, so I was filled in on some of the details later.

Yvette and Philippe were with me as my contractions began to build. We knew it was time. My water never broke, but the intensity of my contractions increased, and they became closer together in time. Philippe had been studying a book on home births and followed each step to help coach me through the process. Yvette was reassuring me that all was happening as it needed to. However, once I had the urge to push, Yvette checked for the baby's head. She looked shocked and almost disturbed. I didn't know how to interpret her reaction.

Philippe went outside to get advice from Jacques, who said that the bag had not broken. Philippe needed to break it so the baby could come out. He used his finger as a hook and water gushed out, along with Dominic, who slipped into

Philippe's hands. But just as he felt some relief that the hard part of the birth was over, he looked up to find me convulsing as if in a seizure. I'm not sure how long I was in that state, but somehow, I came to and was able to hold my baby for the first time.

After 20 hours of labor, my baby had finally arrived. We all thought we'd made it out of the woods.

But I was troubled by the fact that he would let out these large gasps of air. He also wasn't nursing, which seemed like a bad sign. Many first-time mothers can relate to the struggle of latching their baby for the first time, but he just didn't seem to have the primal reflex to even suck. All night I lay by my newborn, hearing him continue to gasp for air. Something seemed wrong. He was never fully awake or asleep. It was more like an unconscious state.

Philippe didn't know what to do any better than I did, so he went and got his parents to come and look at Dominic. They thought Dominic was probably just really exhausted after a difficult birth. He probably just needed to rest, they said. They seemed so confident, I assumed they must be right.

Several hours went by. Dominic kept letting out a strange screech like he was gasping for air. He still wasn't nursing. Finally, I said, "If I have to walk to the hospital, I'm taking him." So, Philippe drove us to the hospital in Chico, which was almost 45 minutes from Paradise.

I remember driving there, holding Dominic in my arms (back then, special car seats weren't mandatory for babies) and thinking about how after a doctor checked him out,

I could go home and put all his new little clothes on him. That's what I thought was going to happen.

But as soon as we walked into that hospital in Chico, we were met by the doctor on staff. He grabbed Dominic out of my arms and said, "I'm so tired of you hippies bringing in these babies born at home for me to fix." Those words were powerful because up until that point, I still thought I was doing everything right. As that ignorant 20-year-old, I really thought I was doing what was best for my baby. They took Dominic away for treatment, and Philippe and I sat in the waiting room for what seemed like a long time. Finally, a nurse said, "Okay, you can see him." When I walked in the room, he was lying in an isolation chamber and had IV tubes in his head. They told us he was in a coma and had been in one since the moment he was born. He had not eaten in 24 hours and was struggling to breathe. I felt like a horrible mother.

When Jacques and Yvette arrived sometime after, they exclaimed, "What have you done? He could get brain damage because they're giving him oxygen!" My head was spinning. What the heck was I doing? I felt there was a war within myself, a debate between Western traditional medicine and alternative medicine over which would win control of my belief system. (This war is still going on.) The more I heard from the doctors or my in-laws, the more I doubted everything, even my own intuition.

What was I doing to my baby? I thought I was doing all the right things, but obviously I wasn't. So, I had to take that information from them, and from the doctor, and think, "All right, I really don't know what to do." I just kept surrendering and praying.

I remember sitting in that room by myself at one point, watching over Dominic, and this nurse came up to me. She put her hand on my shoulder and she said, "It's going to be okay. You don't understand why he's come into your life and why all of this is happening, but it's going to be okay. And one day you will know why." This was the first time anybody had given me any words of reassurance during this whole experience, as I had just kept getting hit with "What have you done? What have you done?" But this woman finally gave me words that felt like they were from God.

So, when it was time for us to leave, I really wanted to thank this woman. I went out to the lobby and asked about the nurse. I said, "I'm looking for a nurse who helped me earlier. She was black." They said, "There's not a black nurse on staff here."

"She put her hand on my shoulder and said, 'This child will teach you so much, this experience is meant to happen, and one day you will understand,'" I told them. And they said, "Well, maybe she came from another ward or something." I've always believed that woman was an angel, giving me the words I needed then.

Dominic was in a coma, and I slept in a chair by his crib for several days, too worried to leave his side. After the fifth day, Philippe convinced me to come home to his sister's house to have food, a shower, and a real night of sleep. At the dinner table, Philippe's family had a discussion with his cousin's wife about her pregnancy. She was close to her due date and confessed some of her fears given what we had just experienced with our home birth. Yvette assured her things would be fine but asked, "You didn't eat any grapefruit in the first trimester, right?!"

Even though it was not directed at me, Yvette had criticized me for eating grapefruit during my pregnancy, so it felt like an insinuation of what I'd done wrong. Lost in my own despair, all I could do was walk out of the room and sit alone on my sister-in-law's bed to try and clear my head. I was speechless and numb.

That night as I slept, I had a dream that I was carrying my baby through a cold hospital-like building. The walls were white, and I turned into what seemed to be a hospital room. A small bed was up against the wall, and I saw a little girl with a gigantic head. I had never seen anything like it, and it shocked me awake. Feeling stunned, I tried to keep the image from my mind, but it was so vivid, it still haunts me to this day.

When it was time to leave, it was not because Dominic was coming home but because the Chico Hospital was not equipped to do anything more for him. So, they flew my newborn baby to the Sacramento Hospital in a helicopter. As we drove to meet him, I kept thinking, "I am going to wake up, and this is going to be a bad nightmare." For the entire 90-minute drive, I kept seeing myself holding my baby, nursing him, and imagining all this as if it were in the past. I can only imagine how my mother lived through two stillborn babies, one right after the other. She is such an inspiration to me, the way she kept her faith in God through it all.

When they admitted Dominic to the hospital in Sacramento, the doctor said that his vital signs looked much stronger than what they'd indicated in Chico. After a total of 14 days, he finally came out of the coma.

When Dominic was released, his discharge papers stated, "possible brain damage." I remember looking at my mom and asking, "Mom, what am I going to do?" She said, "You are going to embrace this with faith and grace."

One true blessing was that at the end of those 14 days, Dominic could actually breastfeed. I was completely engorged with milk the entire time, but my grandma made hotcakes and put them on my breasts to help relieve the pressure and pain. I kept my milk so that when he was finally able to eat, I breastfed him, which was a real blessing with all the different things he had going on.

Months later, once the dust seemed to settle from Dominic's birth, I developed some photographs from my mother's visit. Yvette flipped through the baby photos with me as we oohed and aahed. But when we came across one photo of my mother giving Dominic his first bath immediately after he was born, Yvette reacted with strong opinion. "Why would you give him a bath?! His skin needs to have the afterbirth on him as long as possible!" Immediately, my joy over the memory of his first bath after his birth changed into fear that I had caused another injury to my child. Did this cause his brain damage? My mind wandered, festering again with guilt.

Once we got out of the hospital, I wanted to get out of California as well. I felt betrayed by myself and my new family. I couldn't trust what anyone was telling me, and I wanted to get away. Whether it was a good decision or a rash decision, I just knew I did not want to be there. My husband was a woodworker and built boats, so he answered an ad to go to Minnesota to build a boat. We relocated there from Chico when Dominic was about six months old.

On our way to Minnesota, we stopped by my hometown of Muncie, Indiana. While visiting my mom, we noticed that Dominic would make small movements that looked involuntary, like a twitch or a jerk. At one point, my mother laid him on the floor on a blanket and left him there for a few minutes. When she came back into the room, he was gone. Of course, she panicked, "Oh my gosh! How could I lose my first grandchild?" Finally, she could see the skirt of the sofa moving slightly, and there was Dominic under the sofa, smiling. His jerking movements had caused him to scoot under there. At the time, neither of us knew what that movement was.

THE SEIZURES START

For the brief time we were still in California, Dominic had seemed like a normal baby. But by the time we moved to Minnesota, it was recommended that since he had suffered some injuries at birth, we should probably take him to a chiropractor and get adjustments.

One chiropractor told me that he might get worse. I mentioned his weird twitches, and he said, "These are probably some form of seizure. We're going to work on doing cranial adjustments to help with this."

My sister Angie had gotten pregnant just after high school, and she and her new husband, Steve, moved from Muncie up to Minnesota to stay with us until they could find jobs and a place to live. Well, one day Angie and I were in my apartment in Minnesota, and we heard a strange sound in the bedroom, where Dominic was sleeping. We went in to find him, at barely a year old, in a full-blown convulsion. Dominic's little hands were clenched so tight, I couldn't open them, and his mouth was twisted and bloody from biting the inside of it. To this day, I can still hear the thrashing and his rapid breath.

We rushed him to the Mayo Clinic, where they kept him for a week to run tests. I brought a sleeping bag and slept underneath his bed, kind of pushed up against the wall for five days, because I was not going to leave him. Those days in the children's ICU, with all these families struggling with their child's seizures or leukemia, were a story in themselves. One child there started having seizures after he had received his immunization shots.

I was in a state of questioning my decisions, and I watched the other children try different medications to prevent their seizures. At that time, there were only three or four medications to treat seizures, and they all had some horrifying side effects. Then, more medications were prescribed to counteract them. After witnessing other children experience these side effects, I was afraid of putting Dominic through this medication experimentation. I decided to find more natural ways to control his seizures instead.

When the week was up, after all the EKGs and brain scans and all the other tests were run, Philippe and I sat down with the neurologist to hear his diagnosis. "Only 5 percent of his brain is not damaged," the neurologist said. "And we don't know the capability of that 5 percent."

Then he said, "The best advice that I can give you is to find a place for him to live before you fall in love with him too much. It's just going to be harder and harder to give him up and also to be able to take care of him. This child that you're holding in your arms will probably never talk. There is no way he is ever going to college or prom or going to drive. I'm just telling you the story of your future." That was a lot to digest, especially at age 21. How could he say "before you fall in love"? I'd had my baby for a year, so of course I was in love. But I still wanted to pursue this in the most natural way. So, when the neurologist said, "If you do decide to keep him with you, then we have to start looking at some seizure medications," I had reservations. Again, this was before Google. It was difficult to research all the pros and cons of what seizure medications did. But I was influenced enough by what I'd already seen in the hospital, and by Jacques and Yvette's holistic approach to health, to know that just addressing the symptoms of the seizures was not the proper way to treat him.

I decided to focus on a healthy lifestyle to try to control the seizures. But that didn't really work. Some days, he had more than 100 seizures. There were times when I felt like I should reconsider. But when I would talk to other parents with children on medications, they would say "Well, my son is now on three different cocktails of medications, and they're still not working. But it did cause enough kidney damage that we had to put him on another medication too." So, that didn't seem like a better solution.

Meanwhile, life continued as it does, and I dealt with things as best I could. This involved keeping a diet diary and constantly researching seizures. We saw Chinese medicine doctors, chiropractors, and anyone else who could have some knowledge of ways to treat seizures. I relied heavily on my faith and prayed constantly for God to heal him.

LEARNING TO FORGIVE (LETTING GO OF INNER JUDGMENTS, BLAME, AND A VICTIM MINDSET)

True forgiveness is when you can say "Thank you for that experience."

—Oprah Winfrey

Philippe tried his best to support the family so I could stay home with Dominic, but our finances were not good. I had to figure out a way to help with our income, and since there was a restaurant very close to where we lived, I got a job there as a hostess. I would go to work when Philippe got home so he could stay with Dominic. There was this one guy, John, who would always come to the restaurant, and we would talk when I seated him at his table. "How are you? Do you live around here? What do you do?" Just those kinds of things.

I came to find out that this guy was a construction worker, and he was getting ready to start a new job, which meant he wasn't going to be living in this area anymore. He said, "I'd love to be able to call you sometime." I said, "Sure."

I gave the guy my number, and he did call me. Back then, we had two phones plugged in at our home, which meant that two people could be on the same phone line and listen. So, my husband and I both answered the phone at the same time when John called. I said, "Oh, I have it."

Then I felt guilty, so I told him, "I am so sorry. I should have never given you my phone number. I'm married. I have a child. And I don't know what I was thinking."

He said, "You just seem like you're really, *really* hurting."

I said, "Yeah, I am." And that phone call turned into something like a counseling session. It just felt so good to talk because I had never shared any of this stuff with my coworkers or anyone in my family.

Near the end of the call, he suggested that we get together for a cup of tea or something. At that time, I was selling Avon and Tupperware, too—anything I could possibly do to help with income. I lied to my husband and said I was going to do a Tupperware party, and I went to meet John instead. This is something that I am not proud of.

We just sat and had tea and talked. He told me that he had a girlfriend and that she knew he was meeting with me. "This girl I met," he said he had told her, "she needs somebody to talk to." This made it all feel more innocent. But I had lied to my husband, so it really wasn't that innocent on my part.

John told me he had gone through his own experience that had led to him becoming an alcoholic. His house was broken into when he was 16 years old, and his brother was shot and killed in front of him. He turned to alcohol after that and eventually started going to Alcoholics Anonymous. Through AA, he was able to become the person who could share with me his secret for being able to move on.

Basically, he gave me the best advice. He said, "I know that right now you're feeling like a victim, like this happened to you and that your husband and your in-laws did this. But they didn't. Nobody did this. This was just an experience. And it's important for you to look at yourself in the mirror and say, 'I forgive you' and to look at your husband and tell him, 'I forgive you.' Whether they feel like it's their fault or not, it doesn't matter. You need to say, 'I forgive you' to all of them."

He told me that if I didn't, it was going to eat me up alive. I thought about it, and I decided he was right.

One day not long after this, my husband came home from work and found me in the corner, holding our son and just rocking back and forth and crying. I just kept saying,

"I need help." I don't know what I was thinking, because I couldn't remember any of this when Philippe told me about it afterward.

But he saw that I did need help, so he called his parents and said, "Selina is losing it and I think that she really needs a break." I then flew out to California with Dominic to stay with Jacques and Yvette so they could help me through this. I stayed for three weeks. Yvette would cook all the meals, which was a wonderful treat. Jacques would help care for Dominic and connect me with people who offered therapies for him. Cynthia would drive us to San Francisco three times a week to see an old Chinese acupuncturist who worked points on Dominic in hopes of reversing the brain damage and alleviating his seizures. He also gave him very potent-smelling herbs.

While I was gone, my husband read my diary, probably to try to get a better idea of what I was going through. But in it, I had poured out everything about meeting with John. I wrote: *I feel so guilty. I don't even know if I still love my husband. I don't know if I care for this guy. I was wrong for using someone else to get through these feelings, but I think God works in mysterious ways, and whatever experience this guy had gave him the gift to help me turn my victim and guilt thoughts into thoughts of forgiveness.*

When I got back, Philippe said, "I'm so sorry, I read your diary. But I would do anything to keep you." He wanted to know what he could do to make this different. So, I agreed to work on our marriage, which is how Carla, my eldest daughter, came into this world. I'll go more into that episode in the next chapter.

I called the construction worker to tell him that I couldn't see him anymore, but he suggested we talk in person, so we met up for lunch. At lunch, he told me that he couldn't see me anymore because his feelings were getting stronger, and it wasn't healthy. He didn't want to ever split up a family.

I told him, "Well, I need to stop seeing you, too, because my husband read my diary and I really need to get my act together. I should use my husband as my sounding board instead of going to an outsider." And that was it. I never saw that guy again. Writing about this now, I find myself thinking more about toxicity, not just in the body but also the mind and the heart. There are experiences and elements of our lives that, if they're not handled properly, if they're not complemented with other elements such as the magic of forgiveness, these things can eat away at us.

I don't think I would be who I am today if God hadn't blessed me with this angel while also protecting me from it being a toxic relationship. Instead, he gave me the words I needed to hear about how valuable forgiveness is and how withholding it doesn't do anything to the person you're holding a grudge against. That's just toxic to your internal self. What this man taught me about the power of forgiveness really prepared me for the next 22 years of marriage, and the next 27 years of having Dominic as my son.

If I hadn't embraced this beautiful magic of forgiveness, I could have become a very bitter and unhappy person by now. But I did embrace it. I looked at Philippe, and I told him that I forgave him. It was so healing to me, even though he didn't understand what I was forgiving him for. I forgave my in-laws, who were unsure why I blamed them. Of course, I now know that none of this was anyone's fault.

The other person I forgave was my father. Growing up, my father left my mom and all five of us children for another woman. There was always an underlying bitterness and resentment for that. It didn't affect my father, but it was still affecting me. What I realized when I met the construction worker was how vulnerable someone can be, and how easy it was to be tempted. So, my heart melted and opened enough to forgive my father.

I realized you can really hold on to a lot of things and say, "That person doesn't deserve my forgiveness." But *you* deserve the forgiveness. You're the one it benefits. Withholding it didn't do anything to anyone else, did not touch or penetrate them at all. But what forgiveness did for me was amazing. It helped me become the person I am today.

Writing this story over 40 years later, I know the woman I am today has a better understanding of what was at play then with everyone's emotions and coping mechanisms. We all found ways to blame someone or something else for the unwanted outcome and injuries that Dominic suffered. Blame helped us rise above the primal instinct for survival, letting us move out of our depression to anger. I am now watching my older daughter going through the same thing I lived through so many years ago. She, too, is finding ways to process her trauma with her own daughter's seizures. But I see now that blame is debilitating, almost as much as depression can be. Forgiving my in-laws, my ex-husband, and myself have been the key components to my deeper healing.

And really, the most important person I had to forgive was myself. It's the battles within us that make us beat ourselves up. We constantly must forgive ourselves for saying the wrong thing or hurting someone's feelings. I had to forgive myself after acquiring the company, too, for wanting to take it to the next level. It took me a long time to realize that there was nothing to forgive. So, tell yourself, "You did your best. Stop beating yourself up!"

LAB RESULTS

Throughout this book, I keep coming back to the idea of a whole salt and a whole life—all the elements of your life and all the elements of a whole salt. What if you could send your life to the lab and see exactly how full it is? It would come back with a composition of elements like an analysis of sea salt comes back. All the components of your life would show up like different elements: the sodium, the chloride, the calcium and magnesium, and the potassium.

What you'd see is that some elements of your life might show up as larger macro elements, but you would have these micro elements as well. In a lab analysis, this might be something as small as 0.0004, which is almost not even detectable. In life, there are experiences you may not even have a memory of that still impact the whole of who you are. I think my experience with the construction worker was kind of like this. These small moments are the "micronutrients" essential to a "whole life."

Before we had the more recent lab analysis done, I had been in many debates with different professionals and with customers asking for more detailed information about these salts. "Now how much sodium is in it, and how much chloride is in it, and how do you know how much calcium is in it?" I wasn't completely confident in my answers, and as the company grew, so did the questions.

I knew that we couldn't be certain about the salt unless we had another test run, one that analyzed the salt on its own, not including the water, like the one Jacques had done back in the early '70s.

Jacques was respected and trusted because he'd written the first book to teach people about sea salt. But thinking strategically, as we moved forward with the company, it only made sense to bring more credibility to the education we offered with a scientific, third-party lab analysis to back up Jacques' claims. If we could take all of Jacques' educated theories from his book and turn them into credible data with the lab analysis, then the proof would give us the strategic advantage in the salty wars.

We could also compare that profile when searching for new salt sources, as well as potentially laying the wet versus dry debate to rest, and the grey versus white or pink debate as well.

So, in 2019, we invested $19,000 in a full 72-elemental analysis on all the salts we carry. There was some concern that the composition might not match with Jacques' understanding. It might turn out that the salt wasn't really as good as we thought. But we had to know for certain.

Each salt has nuances of texture and flavor, and a different mineral profile, but more importantly they are all the same in terms of wholeness and completeness.

And the pH was even more alkaline than we expected! Now, with each new salt we are introduced to, we immediately send it to the lab for detailed analysis. We now know what standard to hold a quality salt to, and we know the different ratios of minerals in each different salt.

This knowledge has helped us better inform the customers so they can decide which salt is best for their specific dietary needs. We don't make recommendations, but we provide the information our customers need to decide. One salt may be richer in potassium, another may be higher in sodium and chloride, but all in a form that is absorbable and recognizable by the body.

We've also concluded through analysis that no matter what the moisture content, the salt still holds the same mineral consistency. So, our salt is every bit as nutritious, even if it dries out. Jacques may have been in error about that last part, but through testing we've proven some of his other insights to be even more credible. It all comes down to the importance of all the other elements in a whole salt that allow our bodies to process and assimilate the sodium chloride.

So, why is our sea salt better than table salt? Because it's a whole salt that has all the different elements intact, micro and macro—they're all extremely significant.

I think it's important for customers to see the analyses. You can find them on our website at **www.selinanaturally. com** or call our support line at 1-800-TOP-SALT to learn more about the results.

You almost have to be a chemist to really understand what all the elements in unrefined sea salts are and what they do. But anyone can use common sense to see that if it has this much magnesium, potassium, sodium, chloride, and calcium—and our bodies have a similar amount—then it mimics the composition of our body. Or you can just trust the fact that nature made this whole salt, just like making our whole character—and every single element in that salt is necessary, even if it's the smallest, most minute amount— just like every little component that makes up our lives.

In the next chapter, I'll tell the story of how Philippe and I came to own the company.

4

Embracing Uncertainty: The Company Changes Hands

It is how we embrace the uncertainty in our lives that leads to the great transformation of our souls.

—Brandon A. Trean

JACQUES, MY FATHER-IN-LAW and the founder of the company, passed away in 1994. It all started with the kind of phone call nobody ever wants to get: Jacques had suffered a heart attack, and he was in the hospital. We knew Jacques' medical history and that he was born with a deformed heart valve. Years before, he was in a major car accident that caused his chest to collapse, creating more complications with his heart. He underwent heart surgery to help correct the issues but decided against the anticoagulant medication to help keep his blood from clotting in the new valve.

That morning, he had gone to shovel snow in the driveway when he suddenly fell and went into cardiac arrest. Yvette came to his aid, but by the time the doctors were able to treat him, it was too late. He was in a coma, and on life support. Philippe flew out to California from Palm Beach Gardens, Florida, where we then lived, to be with his mother. After a few days, they realized the only decision was that they should turn off the machines.

After that decision was made and Jacques passed away, Yvette was left with the company to run completely by herself. Almost immediately, she and the company became ground zero for the underhanded. A man who used to work for the company and a few others still within it saw an opportunity to take advantage. He duplicated the member database and started to send out flyers stating that they were The Grain & Salt Society and that they were now changing their name. They even took some of our inventory. Philippe saw all that was happening, so he stayed in California to help his mom with the business.

Meanwhile, I stayed in Palm Beach Gardens with the three children. It was now also my job to check in on Philippe's employees, the woodworkers, and make sure they got paid. I was also cooking macrobiotic meals for cancer patients. Since I was cooking anyway all day long, I would just make these plates and people would come and buy the plates from me. This was in addition to babysitting several children and designing costumes to pay for my daughter's ballet tuition. That's what I was juggling while Philippe was in California helping his mother with all the details that needed to be attended to.

Then, one day, Philippe called and said, "I think that we're going to have to move to California. I really can't leave my mom here like this." And I agreed because Philippe had always been there for my family. Jacques and Yvette were always there for us, and I wanted to help repay them for all their help over the years. So, we packed up our family of five and headed west to start a new chapter of our lives.

SPECIAL NEEDS

Over the past 15 years, from Dominic's birth to the move to California, I had really struggled. I was in denial at the beginning. I even tried to bargain with God. My naïve, younger self would say "Okay, God, I'm going to live my life as clean as I can possibly live it. I am never going to say a cussword. I am never going to do anything bad, and I know you're going to reward me by completely curing Dominic because that's how much faith I have in you."

I even refused to get Dominic a wheelchair because I felt like I would be showing God I didn't have faith. In all the years raising my son, I was a believer of God and went to church, but I wasn't getting the emotional support there that I needed to deal with my situation. I was really hurting, so I started to read books written by Deepak Chopra and

Wayne Dyer—these kinds of people. These books taught me how to take uncertainty and embrace it, as well as how to have faith and trust and all that.

Meanwhile, my sister Angie had gotten a full-time job just weeks after her daughter, Sarah, was born. She needed childcare, so Sarah stayed with me a lot. I was so blessed to have my niece come into my life. She practically lived with us the first five years of her life. I didn't realize until then the reward value when your child reaches typical milestones, how those simple accomplishments of sitting, grabbing things, and baby babbling make the sleepless nights and exhausting days worthwhile. Even a simple smile responding to mine was something I could never take for granted after my experience with Dominic. My child never walked, talked, or returned my love with affection. It was hard emotionally, but Sarah offered some joyous hope to that part of my first-time mothering experience.

With Sarah, I got to watch her excel and progress the way a normal child should. I still love her like she was my own daughter, so it was easy for me to fill that emotional tank. She was born February 2, 1980, and Dominic was born January 1, 1979, so she was just a year younger. And since his food still had to be pureed, I would give Dominic a bite, then give her a bite, and they slept in the same baby bed. Anyplace we would go, she would sit on his lap in the stroller. They were like twins, basically.

So, when Carla was conceived five years later, you would think that would be great news. But I remember going to the doctor and him telling me that I was pregnant, and then I remember driving back with Dominic over a bridge. I just kept thinking that if I drove off this bridge, Dominic and I would both go and nobody would have to take care of him, and I would not have to have the fear of having this second child. I didn't feel worthy enough, or qualified, or whatever you want to call it. I was really scared.

I was reliving the experience of first having so much confidence when I was pregnant with Dominic, but then having that confidence torn apart. I was still fighting wars inside my head, questioning the right and wrong ways of life and what to eat and what not to eat. Go to the doctor versus don't trust the doctor. I was finding my way, finding my strength. And strength doesn't come from comfort. It comes from trials and testing.

When I was pregnant with Dominic, I wrote in my journal: *Please give me a child that is special and when we walk in the room, we will be noticed.* Now, I have no idea what I meant by that. But I got what I prayed for. Dominic came into this lifetime as special as ever. So, I prayed in my journal while I was pregnant with Carla: *God, please let this baby be born with all her physical functions unharmed.*

It took me about three or four months to finally get excited about being pregnant again. And once I could feel movement, I started to fall in love with this new baby who was not born yet. Even though there was still fear there, my faith was kind of overriding the fear. *God loves me so much. It's not going to happen again. This is going to be a beautiful baby. But this time, I'm going to do every single thing that the doctor tells me to do.*

This time, when the doctor told me to eat lots of dairy, I did, even though, in the macrobiotic diet, you don't eat dairy. I got bad migraines, but I kept doing it.

When it was time to deliver the baby, I also did everything the doctors told me to do. The nurse was sitting there with me, and we were chitchatting while I was going through my breathing. Suddenly, the heart monitor around my stomach went down to almost nothing. The nurse then said to me, "This is probably what happened with your first birth."

As soon as she said that, in my mind, I was giving birth to Dominic all over again. I was gripped with anxiety so bad I couldn't breathe. I started to hyperventilate, and I could see the people who were in the room during Dominic's birth. It was horrible, just so weird and eerie. But the nurses and doctors calmed me down, and within minutes they had my gown cut off me, my stomach cut open, and Carla out of there.

When I came to, I said, "I heard somebody counting out loud."

A nurse said, "Carla's cord was wrapped around her neck, and as they unwound it, everybody in the room was counting how many times it was wrapped around."

The cord had been wrapped around her neck *four* times, and she was not breathing at all. Philippe passed out because he thought she was dead. It took a while for them to get her to breathe, but she finally did.

I was still trying to process this while recovering from the C-section, and the doctor came in to tell me that Carla's Apgar score was very low. "It's one in two, and it's supposed to be ten, so we really need to keep an eye on this little girl to make sure that she doesn't have any brain damage." How could this have happened again?

I said, "What do you mean? Is she going to be like Dominic? What are you saying to me?"

She said, "We don't know."

I remember the joy of having a brand-new baby erased the fear of what I was being told. But in the back of my mind, I was anticipating every accomplishment to be recognized as a miracle. Every phase in Carla's life, I asked her to do more earlier than expected and encouraged her progress. What I put her through to give me the reassurance she did not have brain damage! I wanted her to roll over when she was two days old. I wanted her to sit up when she was two weeks old. I was so excited just to get her to hold something in her hand. It was like she was winning the Olympics for every teeny tiny thing she did. I was so relieved that her brain was functioning normally.

With Carla, it was almost like God knew I was going to need actual, physical help, and Carla came here like a born caregiver. She was like that from the very beginning. Even at the age of three, she would get the diapers for me. She would always bring me things, and I look at her today and see how this formed her personality. She can pick up on any mood that I'm in or starting to go into, and I can watch her whole being go into how-can-I-make-mom-happy mode. How can I help her?

Thank God she ended up completely normal, but I was embracing uncertainty every day watching Carla. Fast-forward four and a half years to when I started thinking maybe we should have another child. Things were kind of going smoothly. I mean, Dominic was still having his seizures but fewer than before, and I was dealing with it. So, I ended up conceiving another child five years after Carla was born.

While I was pregnant with Colette, I went to the doctor in my first trimester because I started to spot, or bleed, a little. He said, "You should not be picking your son up."

"Yeah, right," I said. "What else am I going to do?"

Most days, I was home alone with the kids while Philippe was at work. So, to give you a visual, this is what I had to do: Dominic sat in a recliner because it was one of the most comfortable seats for him to sit in, with a blanket under him. I would slide the blanket slowly off the recliner to make a smooth transition to the floor. Then I would pull the blanket down the hall to his bedroom and get him on the bed by picking him up under his arms while five-year-old Carla held his feet.

I just kept dealing with everything the best I could, but I worried that I might lose the baby. "Maybe I'm not supposed to have another child," I thought. I would write in my journal: *God, please bring some light and laughter to our family.*

And lo and behold, on June 13, 1989, Colette came out just fine with a planned Cesarean section. When Carla was born, God knew I needed somebody to help with Dominic. "No, Mom, I'll change him. No, Mom, I'll do this." She's still like that. But when Colette came into this world, it was with an attitude of "What can I do to make you laugh?"

Until then, we'd just been existing. There was always the question of "How am I going to get through this?" When Colette came, everything lightened up. She brought laughter into our home. My daughters have blessed me—they are both unique in their own way. Carla would ask me questions like "How does seaweed make your hair grow?" and Colette would ask me "Why did God make junk food taste so good and healthy food taste so bad?" This gives you an idea of their personalities.

Now, I had three children. By then, I had surrendered and put Dominic in a wheelchair, so the kids were all stacked up on it anyplace I went. That's how I got around. I would put the kids anywhere I could on the wheelchair and push it. The only time I had a pity party was when people pitied me. "Oh my God, you poor thing, how do you do this?" Then I would stop to wonder how I was doing it. Otherwise, it was just what I did.

CALIFORNIA, HERE WE COME (BACK)

We started the process of moving to California. We had to sell our house, and we had to figure out how we were going to travel across the country. I left a lot behind: the support network in my neighborhood and my church, Palm Bible

Chapel; my best friend, Gloria, with her four children similar in age to my children; my mom and stepdad; and my sister, who was starting a family. I went, but it wasn't with a smile on my face. I knew it was what we had to do, but I also told myself it would just be for a couple of years. Then we'd come right back.

That's really what I thought when we moved to California. But once I got there, I got pulled into the business quickly. Being involved with it was very interesting to me. The company was in a small building, maybe 2,000 square feet, with five employees at the time. They were just selling salt, and everything was done either by mail order or over the phone. Of course, there was no internet back then.

I started to go in regularly and help Philippe with answering the phones and taking orders. I would bring Dominic in with me every day because I hadn't found a caregiver for him yet. Colette was just starting kindergarten, and Carla was already in the fourth grade, so they would be at school. While I was bringing Dominic into work, one of our employees said, "You know, my sister would probably be a really good caregiver for Dominic." We were so blessed to be introduced in this way to Rita.

Rita worked out so well that I was able to start going to work with Philippe every day. And as I started answering the phones and taking orders, I realized that people weren't just asking for salt. They were asking where they could get things like brown rice or other products that would support a healthy lifestyle change. I knew where to get these things because I'd been eating this way for over ten years now.

So, I started to learn about how we could source these items and bring them in. They would say "Well, how do you cook this stuff?" I started writing up some recipes, and then I started sending them out. Then we realized that The Grain & Salt Society that Jacques had started could use a stronger purpose.

Since there was no longer a salt shortage, we had to figure out how to give the membership value. A newsletter seemed like one way to do that. There were a lot of influential people promoting health and nutrition, and they were promoting our salt when they were doing that. I started contacting them with requests. Can you share an article on fermentation? Can you share an article on omegas? Start-up companies were able to tell their stories about their products in our newsletter.

They started submitting articles, so now we had a newsletter that we sent out four times a year to the thousands of members of the society, filled with articles from other people about nutrition, health in all forms, and spirituality. I realized I really loved what I was doing and that I was pretty good at networking and being a part of a new way of thinking. I felt like I was in my element.

In the middle of all of that, it was always in my head: we're going to go back to the East Coast, so we've just got to figure out how to save enough cash so we can make it a smooth transition. This was to be with or without the business. I just knew I didn't want to settle down in California.

RELOCATING THE BUSINESS

Ultimately, we weren't going back to the East Coast without the company. Philippe and I were invested in the business by then, and we thought that moving the company would be a good thing to do because we would have more of my family's support. We'd started meeting with professionals to get that plan underway, even though at this time Yvette still owned the company 100 percent. We were doing about $125,000 in revenue per year at this point in 1994 and were looking for the best place to grow the company. We started looking for places, anywhere from Florida all the way up to Virginia Beach.

A lot of our customers seemed to be in Virginia or North Carolina, so when I was on the phone taking an order, I would ask them, "What is it like there?" Customers actually started offering, "Well, you can come and stay with us. We'll pick you up at the airport if you want to explore our area." It was fantastic that we were getting all this support.

As we started to explore, one of my customers from Raleigh, North Carolina, invited us to visit, and Philippe and I took him up on it. But it just wasn't a place that gave us any goosebumps or anything. Then we visited Asheville. We couldn't believe how beautiful Asheville was and how much we wanted to live there, which is interesting because a lot of natural product companies have migrated to Asheville, North Carolina, for their own personal reasons. Today it's a saturated natural product manufacturing area.

Yvette was on board with us taking over the company from her. She had reconnected with a boyfriend from her past and wanted to live with him in New Orleans. Philippe and I agreed to split our ownership of the company 50/50. We would meet with an attorney to incorporate in North Carolina and then we would buy Yvette out. The company was doing from $700,000 to $800,000 in revenue at the time in 1997, so Yvette was able to retire with what we paid her.

Deciding where to move was one thing, but we still had to do the move itself. Since we were a mail-order company, we weren't dependent on the local economy or local customers, but there was still some question as to whether we'd be able to survive the move. Our financial counsel and our legal counsel both said, "For a company that is this new, to relocate even across town is very risky. For you to be relocating across the country is almost suicide." The idea was not well received.

But I'd done the math, and I knew we probably needed about $280,000 in cash to be able to do this successfully. Then there shouldn't be any interruption in income if we did it right. We were mail order, so as long as we were ready for the next catalog, we could just tell our customers that there might be a one-week or two-week lag time for getting their products because of the move.

It took two years for us to save enough money to make the move happen. That's also how I learned to deal with my business uncertainties. I learned to research and plan everything out, to be as calculated as possible. Then I jumped into the pool of faith, hoping our plan would work.

We found a building that was just under 6,000 square feet in size, previously owned by an X-ray company, in Asheville. We purchased it and the property, and we parked a motor home out back to stay in. Then we loaded everything up and we moved to North Carolina.

Our whole family of five stayed in that little motor home for over four months. If that wasn't enough of a challenge, we were supposed to take occupancy of the building on a certain date, but the X-ray company could not move out because their new building was not ready yet. We shared that building for almost five months with this other company. We were working in one tiny room, sharing the shipping department and everything else.

It was crazy, but we did it. We started getting our first shipments of salt in, and we had to figure out where it could be packaged. We didn't really have the space, so we bought 40-foot containers and we set up our packaging facility inside them. We put ads in the paper and started interviewing people. I had brought along two people from the company in Paradise, California, to help us with the interviewing and the training.

We realized we needed a whole new software system that supported a database, a mail-order company, and diverse products, so we purchased Mail Order Manager and lovingly named her MOM. I was not computer savvy, so for the first full month we implemented this new software, we sent out three duplicate orders to every single customer. This went on unnoticed for a whole week! If anyone could write a book about business bloopers, I could.

The software had messed up, but we also had all-new employees. They didn't recognize the regular customers or have the radar to notice mistakes—even when we were sending triple orders to the same people! They were just processing orders. That was all exhausting: working in a building with another company, hiring new people, and implementing a new CRM system on all-new computers, all within five months' time. This was one of the most chaotic times in our company history.

Terry Patton was one of our first hires. She had just got out of high school and, when she went home after her first day, she said, "I think they're a real company because they had brand-new computers all opened up and everything and they were getting ready to install them, so I think they're pretty legit." She ended up being a valuable employee and designed our first website and everything that went with it. What I love about her first impression is that to me everything didn't even seem real somehow, but she thought, "Yeah, they must be a real company because they have computers."

We had to hire about seven new people in total. Once the X-ray company moved out, it felt like we could move around.

Then everything seemed to be going much more smoothly. We printed everything: our labels, and our newsletter, which we just stapled together. All the work was done in-house.

It was still a small building, so we had everybody in the same room. I was in the same room with the sales department, and that was a joke, too, because I would hear them talking to a customer and I'd run over to the phone and say "No, don't say that. Say this." Gosh, what a training it was! I felt like a helicopter mom. Being a Cancerian, I would over-hear a sales team member mention a sweet old lady on the other side ordering a pound of salt, and I would say "Oh, don't charge her, send that for free." Eventually, our sales team thought it would be best if my office wasn't in the salesroom. They needed to make sales! My sister, who is also our CFO, still keeps me in check to this day so I don't "give away the farm."

We understood that there was a big opportunity at that time. Remember, this was still before the internet and Amazon. Marketing back then was done very differently. Our sales growth happened purely on word of mouth. Doctors and customers told their friends about us and really did the marketing for us since they were already our biggest fans.

But I wanted to expand with more products, bringing them in and testing them. So, I found people knowledgeable about sourcing and purchasing, and we hired them. They knew how to bring products in, talk to vendors, and get the best prices and everything.

We continued writing our newsletter, but we started tailoring it more toward our new products. So, if we brought a new product in, like sauerkraut, we would have the owner of the sauerkraut company write an article about sauerkraut and how important it was, how it supported the intestinal flora, and how fermentation is so good for you. We might also have them write about their company, how they started it and why, and what the values of their products were.

We eventually had over 3,000 other products from other vendors at one time. We still also brought in doctors and other professionals to talk about health and nutrition. Giving these start-up companies an opportunity to tell their stories and sell their products at the same time was very fulfilling for me. It was really my element. I felt so blessed to be a part of this company, continuing Jacques' legacy. In the next chapter, I'll take you around the world on my search for new salts.

5

Salty Adversity: The Search for New Sources

There is a supply for every demand.

—Florence Scovel Shinn

BY 2004, my marriage to Philippe had ended in divorce. I bought him out and became 100 percent owner of the company. I was now in debt almost a million dollars and had to go out and start the relationships with the salt suppliers myself. Before this, Philippe was the one who would communicate with our salt suppliers in Brittany, and I had anxiety about how I would be perceived as the new owner, especially as I did not speak French at all.

So, I was apprehensive when I set out for Brittany for my first trip as full owner. Before I left, I reached out to Vincent, an attorney in Belgium whom I'd met a year or so before in San Francisco, where he and his partner were doing business. He was another one of God's angels I was going to need. I asked him if there was any way he could help me establish this new relationship with the salters. He said, "Absolutely." So, I flew into Belgium, where I stayed with Vincent and his wife. Then he and I drove to Brittany. We used the three-and-a-half-hour drive to discuss all the details about how to present ourselves. He was going with me not so much in the capacity of an attorney but more as a translator to help me out. I needed to fully understand the potential relationship opportunities with the salt suppliers and if they were going to accept me in this new role.

When we arrived at the salt flats in Brittany, Vincent helped me immensely with translating and building the necessary relationships. The salters seemed excited to receive me, and at the end of the day, there was really no issue. At the time, my company was their biggest customer, so of course they would still want to do business with me. Today, I have strong relationships with all our salt suppliers.

OTHER BRITTANY SOURCES

But what if the salters *hadn't* been willing to do business with me? Once that fear was behind me and I knew that I could continue business with these suppliers, I also knew that I needed to diversify my sources. Getting everything from one source seemed too risky. It left the company vulnerable.

First, I looked for other suppliers in the region. I found another salt source through a chef named Holly Peterson in Northern California. She had contacted me and wanted to see how we could increase our volume demand. Sylva Laduce, the owner, was a true salt master. I also found yet another salt source in the same region of Brittany. Ultimately, I was able to build relationships with the cooperative with the help of a broker named Betty Adams and with three other different suppliers in the same Brittany region. We were now more diversified within the region with these three sources that we're still doing business with today. So, if something happened to one of the sources, then we still have two others. But what if something happened to the entire region?

I was explaining my goals to Betty when she said, "Well, I'm a broker for a salt in Portugal too. It's a beautiful fleur de sel. I would love to meet you there. We can go and explore, and you can meet the supplier. He's a fifth-generation person who's been harvesting for all these years."

I thought that sounded great, but I also had my reservations. Jacques had always been so adamant about the grey salt. The suppliers in Brittany told me, "You will not get the same quality of minerals from the salt in Portugal. It is too hot, and there is not enough time to allow the minerals to be produced in the quick evaporation. The clay is the only way to get the mineral composition you are looking for in your Celtic Sea Salt brand."

BEYOND BRITTANY: DON'T JUDGE A SALT BY ITS GEOGRAPHIC LOCATION

Starting with Portugal, I set out to find other salts with the same features and benefits as the original light grey Celtic Sea Salt. My curiosity propelled my journey to venture out and explore more, despite my "small-town girl" insecurities of not knowing the world. I was about to discover a side of myself I never knew I had. I traveled to other countries to meet strangers and build business relationships in hopes of growing this small business to what I knew it could become.

Using what knowledge I had from our original source, I inspected the new sources with a critical eye to find a quality high-mineral salt. With every new country and new farmer, I became wiser and more decisive about how to improve conditions to limit potential contamination, about quality storage facilities, and about better work environments for those working in the fields. I was paving a new way to farm salt using sustainable fair-trade practices by spreading the knowledge of the Brittany practices I had learned initially.

I explained to my lab guy, Carl Nelson from ENC Labs, that I wanted to find more sources, but the salts from these sources had to have the same composition as the Light Grey Celtic Sea Salt or close to it. I said, "I'll be sending you several different salts so that you can help me out with this." We would then talk about the results of the analysis and together determine if the salts were up to the standards of the Celtic Sea Salt from Brittany.

The lab analysis was just the first step for doing my due diligence in researching new sources. Carl would test the mineral composition, as well as any heavy metals or contaminants. But that was just the first puzzle piece to knowing whether I wanted the new salt. What if children were being exploited to farm the salt, for example? I had to travel to each location to ensure the farms were sanitary and treated their workers well. Now we call these standards Good Manufacturing Procedures (GMPs).

My goal was to find salts with a beautiful healthy composition while also keeping to sustainable farming methods. I was pleasantly surprised at what other countries offered as I grew my explorations globally.

THE HIMALAYAN CRAZE

It's not like I hadn't looked into other salts before. I think it was in 1995 when I came across an article in *Reader's Digest* about a Himalayan salt. It was a pink salt from the Himalayas that was supposed to be low in sodium and rich in minerals. I thought it sounded interesting.

So, I ordered some of the Himalayan salt from Pakistan, and they sent me all kinds of things with it. I mean, the shipping alone cost almost $400 because it wasn't just a little sample of salt. They sent me soap dishes, candle holders, and Himalayan salt lamps all carved out of this rock salt. Everything from powdered salt to these great big rocks that were about three inches in diameter. My team and I looked at one another puzzled, asking, "They are eating this rock?" Some of the salt was white, some really dark pink, and some light pink. I was intrigued.

This was before there were any Himalayan salt lamps in the United States, so this was a whole new thing. It was pretty, but it seemed more like a novelty, and that's not what our company was about. We were looking for a salt that most closely mimicked our body's plasma of minerals, with potassium, magnesium, calcium, sodium, and chloride.

I sent a sample of this salt to the lab, just to see. The results came back, saying it was 97.63 percent sodium and chloride, as compared to Celtic Sea Salt, which was only 85 percent sodium and chloride. I thought, "Well, there are really not a whole lot of significant minerals here. It's very rich in sodium and chloride but not the other vital minerals we now know make a healthy salt." It was not up to Celtic Sea Salt standards. Would Jacques have chosen to add this salt to our lineup? But since it was so pretty, I put it aside and gave a lot of it away as gifts.

Then, almost overnight, the phone started ringing. I would say probably four out of every five calls that came in were from people asking if we knew anything about this Himalayan pink salt. I do know the raw-foods movement people really jumped in and started to promote it to their community, and it went viral. But I couldn't believe it. People would say "Oh, it has 82 minerals and trace minerals, and it's just amazing." I would say "Well, do you have the analysis? I would love to be able to see what you're talking about." But nobody could provide me one.

I even wondered if maybe there was another Himalayan salt that they were talking about that had all these amazing properties. So, I found two other sources, and I sent those to the lab also. But they came out the same. I could not understand what the big thrill was. I thought it was going to be a fad. But, of course, anybody reading this book today has heard of Himalayan salt. That is how it hit our market share without evidence-based analysis to support its mineral-content claims. Should I have adopted Himalayan salt just because there was such a high demand for it? Maybe, but it would have conflicted with our mission to provide unrefined sea salt, which has better flavor and texture, has a better mineral profile, and is sustainably harvested rather than mined. Also, when I researched the possibility of visiting the salt mines, the word was they were not safe places to go.

PORTUGAL FLEUR DE SEL

The Algarve area of Portugal was my first launching pad into exploring another country's salt production. I was nervous, excited, and very grateful to have Betty, the salt broker, to help guide me and translate. In all the juggling of operations for the business, settling into the new building, and being a newly single mom, my head was spinning a little with all the plates I had to balance. Without an assistant to help keep things organized, I booked my own travel as well.

A week before I was set to meet Betty in Lisbon, she called me, asking where I was. I told her I was sitting at home in my room. I was puzzled at first by her question, only to be horrified at the realization I had booked my flight one week later than hers! Not only was I embarrassed by this amateur mistake, but I was also faced with the terrifying thought that I would now have to embark on my trip alone, without her help.

When I arrived in Portugal the following week, the salt farm owner, Rui, picked me up. He was an older man who spoke broken English, so I knew right away communication would be a challenge. He drove me in his truck to a remote town where the salt flats were. I learned quickly that the more remote the town was in Europe, the less the local people spoke English. I settled into my room, and the next morning Rui picked me up and gave me a tour of his salt flats. They were not only beautiful but also set up in a similar way to the Brittany flats with very clean harvesting practices.

The following morning, Rui was busy, so I had the day to myself. The hotel had a few bicycles parked by the front door, so I gestured to the front desk clerk and asked in my tourist way if I could borrow a bike. He seemed to agree, so I set off to explore the other salt flats I noticed outside of Rui's area. I wanted to understand what other salt farmers were doing and producing in the area.

With each turn, I went deeper into a maze of endless salt flats. Many were positioned up against what seemed like sewage processing plants. This really highlighted for me the quality of Rui's flats. They were nothing like this. The hot day wore on, and I realized I should start making my way back to the hotel. Looking both ways, I realized I wasn't sure which road would take me back. My heart began to race, and I frantically searched for ways to communicate to the locals a need for directions. I remembered I had a brochure of the hotel in my bag, so with a lot of guessing and directions explained in Portuguese, I found my way back to the hotel, so grateful to rest after my first adventure as a solo traveler.

MAKAI PURE

Sometime later, a pharmacist approached me at a trade show—I think it was Expo West. He had a little vial that had maybe 10 cc of a very white salt in it. He said, "I would love it if you could look at this salt and tell me what you think." I said, "Okay, I'll send it to my lab."

When the results came back, my lab guy, Carl, was very surprised. He said, "I am surprised that it's 75 percent sodium chloride. It has so much magnesium and potassium and calcium!" The alkalinity was 10, so it was very, *very* alkaline. There were hardly any impurities. It was almost at pharmaceutical level.

I went back to the pharmacist and said, "I can't believe this salt! Why is it so different?" The secret was that they extracted the water in Kona, Hawaii, from 2,000 feet below the surface of the water, so deep that even sunlight didn't reach it. The water was so cold upon extraction that it could air-condition their building when they ran the water through the vents.

They would bring this water in and put it in salt huts they created, like domes or great big greenhouses. They had a fan to circulate the air so the water would evaporate more quickly. When it did, white crystals formed. My daughter loved the story of how this salt was harvested. I guess she takes after her grandfather Jacques, with his romantic heart, because she came up with the brand name for this perfect salt: Makai, which means "toward the sea." But we'd done such a great job telling people they should only eat Celtic Sea Salt that this new "Makai sea salt" just wasn't selling. We had to shift the label and put Celtic Sea Salt on it. That will be in the next chapter about branding and intellectual property. In the meantime, this salt was an amazing find.

We now had five salt sources in three very different regions of the world. We had three different suppliers in Brittany, we had the fleur de sel from Portugal, and now we had this new deep-sea salt from Hawaii. Once Makai started picking up speed in sales, we soon realized Kona had a limited supply because of the size of its operations. We would either have to invest in growing it or hope to find another source to help supplement the supply.

My lab guy, Carl, introduced me to George, who had a salt company on Molokai, another island in Hawaii. It was a very small, sleepy island, beautiful and secluded, with open countryside and empty beaches. I went there with my daughters to see their operations. The lab analysis showed very similar ratios and purity levels to the salt from Kona. I was stunned because the island of Molokai did not have the same deep drop-off point into the sea right at the beach like Kona did.

Also, while the operations there were smaller than on Kona, the system produced almost the same volumes. The company filtered surface seawater through a powerful filtration system and then built boxes with medical-quality materials to evaporate the water. They could then scoop the crystals into bins, bag them up, and ship them to me. It was perfect. So, now I had two impressive sources to keep our growing Makai brand happy and healthy.

CHALLENGES IN HAITI

I was contacted by four stockbrokers from New York City about salt in Haiti. Two of them were from the island, and their grandmother had passed away and left them some property, which included some saline, salt-harvesting land. It was their dream and vision to give back to their homeland by creating a natural resource commodity that could make the country some money. These men had done a lot of work already and invested a lot of their own money into making sure ports were available for ships to pick up the salt and transport it to the United States.

When they heard about Celtic Sea Salt, they thought maybe the company would want to sell their salt. I said, "Well, send me a sample." They did, and I did my whole due diligence, and I was again blown away by how similar it was to our Light Grey Celtic Sea Salt. So, now it was time for me to explore Haiti.

Once I got to the salt-harvesting area in Haiti, I saw there were a lot of changes that needed to be made in the actual production. It was so hot where the salt was harvested that workers had to arrive just before the sun came up and then get off the salt flats by 11 a.m. It was just too hot to work in the middle of the day.

They would harvest the salt by raking it to the side of the salt pond, but when there was afternoon rain, the salt they'd raked would dissolve right back into the pond. So, there were some things we had to do right away, like build some pole barns, which is just a roof with four poles. That way, they had somewhere to store the salt, so it didn't just dissolve.

The beautiful thing about Haiti was that, as miserable as the heat was and as hard as the labor was to harvest the salt, people worked with big smiles while singing. It felt good to think I could both provide an amazing salt to our salt lovers while also doing something for this community. My heart was there.

I invested quite a bit of money in building a warehouse to ensure we could start harvesting the salt, packaging it, and getting it ready to export to the United States to my facility. We put an ad in the paper for the 12 positions we had open, and over 500 people lined up outside to apply. We were almost ready.

It took us years to set up enough operations to finally bring the salt in, but eventually we did. We were able to bring it in for some customers who were using it as an ingredient salt. But then a lot of things happened. There was the earthquake in Haiti, for one. Then some people stripped the warehouse pipes out of the concrete and stole all our supplies and equipment. We had hired guards, but they got paid off. The location next to ours was a school bus lot, where they even stripped the school buses.

I couldn't continue to invest in Haiti. I had to put that aside and just pray it could possibly come back. I would have loved to bring salt from Haiti again, but there were too many obstacles at the time, and I didn't have the resources to continue.

GUATEMALAN GOURMET

I was contacted by a salt broker in Guatemala named Rick. He said, "I have this amazing salt that I've discovered in Guatemala, and I'd love to send you some samples." He did, and it was 80 percent sodium chloride and very alkaline. It was beautiful and white. So, now it was time for me to explore Guatemala.

The two salt property owners were a married couple, Juan and Imana, and they invited me and my daughter Colette into their home. It was such a beautiful location in the tropics, with the windows of the house overlooking the salt flats, so when you got up in the morning, you could see the salt workers coming in and all of them working.

But there were still conditions I thought should be improved, such as workers being barefooted when they harvested the salt. I said, "They should wear rubber boots to keep things more sanitary." They were also using the same tools for multiple purposes around the land. I told them, "You can't reuse those tools." Small improvements provided places for them to store their salt-harvesting tools and the boots that were only to be worn in the salt ponds. We had to do a little bit of cleaning up in Guatemala.

I was curious how they were able to bring the salt in without a filtration system, but they had one after all. It was the mangroves on the island that filtered the water coming through them before it went into the salt flats. In France, filtration occurred through a labyrinth of clay ponds.

That's how we found our Guatemalan salt, which is marketed as our Gourmet Kosher.

COLIMA CLEANUP

The first time I saw the salt flats in Colima, Mexico, I said, "Oh, this is just not acceptable for an edible salt." I was very impressed with the lab analysis, but when Mariano showed me around the premises, the first thing I noticed was a pole barn that was accessible to animals. There were dogs walking around on the salt and everything. There was a smell, too, like that of a wet bathing suit, which I knew meant there was stagnant water. This would not produce good salt.

I sent Mariano a lot of different recommendations detailing what needed to be done, like removing the plastic from the salt beds. He made all the changes, and then he contacted me. "Okay, Selina, I've made all the changes. I think the salt is up to your standards." He sent me pictures showing the new warehouse he had moved operations into, as well as how the seawater was now filtered through five feet of sand before it got to the salt ponds. Everything was now up to par, so today we're doing business with Mariano from Colima also. He's such a sweet man. He has a little shrine with our Celtic Sea Salt in his house, and he tells me he lights a candle next to it every single day to pray for us. I feel like I've built such amazing relationships with these people also.

A GROWING MOUNTAIN FILLED WITH SALT?

Mariano in Colima told me about a very dear friend of his in Spain. "I think that you'd be very interested in this salt that he has. It's a rare salt, unique compared to all the other salts in the way it's made." The lab analysis wasn't off the charts with good mineral content, but it was very pure, and it had a really good story.

Over two thousand years ago, the Mediterranean Sea had flooded over the land, and then it receded back over the course of years and years. But when it did recede, there was a pocket of ocean water that got trapped underneath the mountains.

They access this water by simply opening a big pipe that lets the briny water gush into salt flats. It's like an underground river of ancient ocean water that they can let in. The water itself has an amazing profile. So, they let this water into salt ponds, where it evaporates to produce a beautiful salt.

I really struggled with this choice. Would Jacques really be against me bringing in a cave salt? After being on location in Spain, I saw this was not a rock salt that is mined but rather a river hidden under a mountain that replenished the salt more rapidly than an ancient mine bed. Each time it rains, the water pressure pushes the mountain up so that the salt source is constantly growing. This helped me feel at ease about the sustainability factor when considering this salt.

We brought this salt into the United States, with about 15 different skews of flavors, and we are looking to see how we can market it, which I'll talk more about in the chapter about intellectual property.

While we were in Spain visiting these different underground springs, I was introduced to the Salt Mountain. I wasn't open to looking at a mined salt because of my sustainability standards, until they showed me the mineral profile. This salt was very, *very* high in potassium, and potassium is sodium's best friend. It helps our bodies assimilate the salt properly and distribute it within the cells.

That intrigued me. *Well, it's naturally occurring potassium, so why don't I go look at it?* So, I went to the cave, and it was like walking into a salt hut, with these gorgeous salt-sicles just dripping from the ceiling. It had a beautiful pink color from the iron within the mountain.

So, after really praying about this, and considering the mineral content and amazing flavor, we are currently in the process of designing the package to sell this new pink cave salt in. I think these new salts from Spain are going to be well received. The packaging is completely biodegradable, and the pink salt is high in potassium and lower in sodium than table salt.

My struggle in deciding about the new salts wasn't just about what Jacques would have wanted but also about preserving the brand integrity. What is Celtic Sea Salt? What does it mean? And what is intellectual property?

In the next chapter, I will talk more about Jim Cockman, who mentored me in some of this. He was a brand master when it came to intellectual property. He counseled me about what it meant to have a brand, and how important it was to make sure you kept the integrity and the brand promise.

So, with all these new, beautiful salts that I'd gone out and found, how could I bring them all in under the Celtic Sea Salt brand? This was the question I would need to answer moving forward.

In the meantime, if you want to know more about the different salt sources and the way the salt comes to us, you can go to the website: **www.selinanaturally.com/faqs** or **www.selinanaturally.com/company**. You may find this interesting if you want to know more about the process.

6
Intellectual Property and Brand Promise

A brand is the set of expectations, memories, stories, and relationships that, taken together, account for a consumer's decision to choose one product or service over another.

—Seth Godin

I WAS NOW embarking on a new journey as a naïve business owner. No longer having my husband by my side, I had to make relationships with other CEO-type people, most of whom were men. Some were wolves in sheep's clothing, but God allowed my path to cross with a man named Jim Cockman, who had nothing but good intentions. He was my angel and helped guide me in my next steps to lead this company and brand.

Jim told me, "You can either build a salt company that's just a commodity and sell it to customers with no brand on it or you can build a company that is a commodity that has intellectual property." It was because of him that I chose the second option to build the Celtic Sea Salt brand.

MY MENTOR

Before I met Jim, I was working with different business consultants here and there. Every now and then, someone would meet me and say "Oh, I can consult for you." Then I'd bring them in to audit the company and see where we should focus our improvements. One business consultant told me there was somebody I really needed to meet, but he kept this guy in his back pocket as leverage without introducing me.

Soon enough, a great friend and mentor of mine, Michael Cianciarulo, who was the president of Earth Fare at that time, told me, "There's this guy you need to meet. His name is Jim Cockman. He's one of the shareholders of Earth Fare, and he's really a brand expert." I came to find out later that this was the same guy my consultant was holding back.

Michael arranged an introduction and a meeting at Jim's house, just outside Greenville. So, I drove out from Asheville with my marketing director and my business consultant to meet him. Jim and his wife, Cathy, lived on this beautiful ranch with all these horses. A dynasty is what it looked like. We met him in his office, where there were all these pictures of him with U.S. presidents on the walls. I mean, this man really knew his stuff.

So, I told Jim our story. I gave him some of our salt and showed him the label. He looked at it and said, "Interesting." Then, he was very upfront about the business side of things. "Well, I'm selective in the clients I bring on. Right now, my rate is about $5,000 a day."

I said, "Wow. Okay." I wasn't expecting that. Of course, there was no way that was going to work. Elizabeth, my marketing director, said, "Well, would you take payment in salt?" He kind of laughed. He thought that was cute.

We left Jim's house that day a little disappointed. But I was honored to have met him and, gosh, what a dream come true to ever be able to work with him!

So, you can imagine my surprise when he called me the next day and said that he and Cathy had prayed about my situation. They wanted to help me for free. "Oh, wow," I said. "You're kidding." He said, "No, I'm not kidding. I want to help you."

Because I knew he was doing me a favor, I was very selective about when I reached out to him. I always wanted to make sure I had a lot of information to give him or plenty of questions saved up to ask him before I reached out. I really didn't take advantage of this beautiful offering as much as I should have, and he realized that too. After about two years of meeting with him just every now and then, he called me. "We need to get together."

During a visit to Tryon, North Carolina, I went for a meeting with Jim, and I brought my assistant and my general manager. We were to meet at Jim's office and then go to eat lunch at a café in Greenville. Jim asked if I would ride with him to the café, and my staff went ahead to meet us there. We were driving along when he suddenly pulled over and turned the car off. He took my hand and said, "Selina, we're running out of time. We need to build this brand. It's import-ant." I agreed.

He said, "So, I'm going to charge you $1,500 a week to build your brand. We have to put a price on this so that you will actually utilize me." He added, "When you move into your new building, we are going to invite all of the top chefs of the world to your grand opening." He was on boards of directors for all these chef institutes, so he had these kinds of connections. This was an amazing offer.

I was scheduled to leave for France in a few days for my first visit since the divorce. Jim said, "When you get back from France, we will start the planning."

This sounded wonderful to me. I was in the process of getting the certificate of occupancy for a new 18,000-square-foot building I was having built so we could move out of the building we were currently doing business in. I expected things to be further along by the time I returned, and then we could focus on the grand opening.

THE 100-YEAR FLOOD

While I was in Brittany, two hurricanes, Ivan and Frances, hit the southern coast of the United States, one right after the other. The amount of rain those two storms sent onto our mountains was historic and caused what is now referred to as a 100-year flood. This flood devastated our little town and wiped out a huge number of homes and businesses. Ours was among them.

"Can't you just go get some wet vacs?" I suggested when my sister told me about the flood over the phone. My sister, the CFO, said, "I am in a canoe right now, and we are looking in the window of the second floor." That was the reality of it. The lower level of the building was completely underwater.

I then spoke with my director of marketing, Elizabeth, and told her I had just met with Jim Cockman. "Call him and see what he thinks we should do."

"He is missing," Elizabeth told me when I called back.

"What do you mean, missing?"

It seemed that Jim had disappeared. So, not only was my building completely flooded but no one knew where Jim was. All this bad news at once was too much. I felt completely blank and didn't know what to do. My mind and body couldn't take it, and I collapsed in an elevator. Luckily, Vincent, my Belgian attorney, was there to catch me and keep me from hitting my head.

This flood had come in, with waves and everything, and demolished the entire warehouse. Because this area had never been flooded before, we had made the call to not get flood insurance. So, here we were, after I had just paid Philippe off and I was still in huge debt for that. (Thank God for my dad loaning me the funds.)

Our total losses came to $468,000 when we put it all on our spreadsheets. I was able to get a FEMA loan at 2 percent interest to pay for it, but only because my sister Theresa, our CFO, was able to itemize every single loss we had incurred. It was an amazing loan, but I was now in debt almost $500,000 with the SBA because of the flood, on top of what I owed for the purchase of the company.

The only thing saved was our server because it was on the second floor, hanging on the wall about six inches above the floodwater line. That was the only saving grace to keep the company going. We had our database, so we could still produce a catalog, contact customers, and all that.

We had been expanding, so our catalog had more than 3,000 products in it, but now we didn't have any of those products in-house. When the news got to the vendors of the products we carried, they started donating products to help us out. We still had to get everything we could out of the flood zone within a certain number of days. The authorities had to quarantine the area, and we wouldn't be allowed back for a certain amount of time.

Because I was still in France, others had to go in and see what they could salvage without me. As my sister told the story, everybody was moaning and complaining, not knowing what to do. So, my sister got up and said, "This is ridiculous. If Selina was here, she'd have rubber boots on, and rubber gloves, and she'd be going out there and just doing what she can." That helped to motivate everyone to start salvaging. We had to at least try to get our paperwork, our bookkeeping, and all of that. My sister Theresa (Teece) and the employees really made it happen. Also, Michael Cianciarulo, the president of Earth Fare, sent some of his employees over to help us with pallets.

When I set eyes on the building again, it looked like it had just been sandblasted with mud and concrete and whatever. I mean, it went all the way up to the ceiling and onto the second floor. I remember some employees coming up and telling me they were good at saving their money. "We just wanted you to know, you don't even have to pay us until you can. Don't worry about it. We love you, and we can make this happen." It was beautiful in all this adversity to see that people were really on our side.

We had been about four weeks away from moving into the new building, already delayed because the power had not been hooked up and turned on. Since this was a newly developed piece of property, I had to have Duke Energy do some extensive installments. The hurricanes that had hit the Gulf caused so much damage, Duke Energy had to relocate all employees to get power back to the affected areas. I remember sitting at my desk in my new office in a building that cost me over $1 million, carrying a divorce settlement that cost me $750,000 with 8 percent interest, three children with a caregiver who cost $2,000 per month, and 26 employees to pay, but with no inventory in stock to fulfill outstanding orders and demands.

I asked God to please help me. If only Jim Cockman was here. As soon as I thought this, there was a knock on my door.

I opened my eyes and looked up to see this tall man with a smile who looked like an angel. He said, "Hi, my name is Cookie, and I would like to speak to the owner of this building." He then told me that the previous week he had received a work order to turn on our power that day, but after the hurricane all such orders had been voided or put on hold. "This morning we were all redirected to hurricane-damaged areas," he said. "But in my prayers this morning, I was called to come here to this address instead."

He asked what I did, and I told him my story. He said, "Well, you must have an angel on your side because this work order would not have been completed for at least four more weeks if I hadn't been called to come here."

Cookie was going to be retiring in a month and he called in some favors to get our power turned on that very day. By 7 p.m. we had power! Afterward, I could get my certificate of occupancy and receive the shipment that was due that week. I believe God inspired Cookie to come and help me. We have been close since.

Philippe stopped by to check on the state of things as well, since he was supposed to get this property. He said, "Can you believe we fought for five years for all of this? And look, now it's all gone." I said, "Yeah, and I'm the one who paid you off, so I'm the one who has the debt with no business now to pay the debt off with."

Meanwhile, Jim still did not turn up. Not being able to get a hold of him made me feel scared and hopeless again. He said he was going to be there to mentor me, but where was he? The more I thought about it, the more I felt there had been something strange about our last meeting. It was like he knew his time was running out.

Finally, the story came out of what led to Jim's disappearance. He was selling one of his SUVs and went to meet a couple interested in buying it. He had an appointment at the bank afterward, but when the bank called his home to see where he was, his wife got worried. "He should be there," she told them. She decided to investigate. She drove over to where he was supposed to meet the couple. Jim's Jaguar was parked there with the door wide open. His wallet and his phone—everything—were right there on the front seat, but the SUV was gone.

I had my marketing manager, Elizabeth, make some flyers and started passing them out while we were trying to get the company back on track. If Jim had been kidnapped, maybe someone had seen something.

MISSING PERSON

Jim Cockman

Jim was reported missing at approximately 11am on Tuesday, September14th.

He was last seen across from The Junction restaurant, at the intersection of highways 11 & 14.

His silver, 1996 Chevy Suburban is missing too. License #FM79075

If you've seen either Jim or his silver Suburban, or have any helpful information regarding Jim's whereabouts, please call...

CRIMESTOPPERS @ 23CRIME (232-7463)

Above is the flyer we made in an effort to find Jim Cockman

Meanwhile, my sister and my staff were provided a storage unit by George Storage. The owner had also been impacted by the flood, and he had a small warehouse with space for people to store pallets of flood salvage. This allowed us to set up another place of operations and get ready for the catalog to be printed on schedule. Vendors were even sending us last-minute products, so we had inventory to ship out. It was so amazing all the help we received.

But later that week, we received a horrifying update on my mentor's whereabouts. They had found Jim's body in a freezer in a warehouse. The kidnapping had gone wrong, and the people who met him about the SUV had murdered him instead.

I remember when I was told they had found Jim's body. I went home and put my face on the ground and implored God, "You're going to have to give me some sort of sign because I can't get up again." I was trying to rise to the challenge of the flood, but this was too much on top of it. I didn't know how to keep going. I didn't have a company. I didn't have any money left because I had just bought my husband out. And now my mentor was gone too. I felt so completely desperate.

That's when God told me, "I take these masters of this Earth with a lot of drama, as you guys would think it would be, just like the way I took Princess Diana and Gandhi and other individuals who have made such an impact. They all left with a huge story, and Jim Cockman was such a profound man. He was a leader and an influence on so many people and such a help. But this is the way I had to take him, and it's okay because his story is being told even more now because of the way he has been taken."

Those words helped me finally get back up. "Okay," I thought. "What would Jim do? He gave you the vision to build this intellectual property, so now you'd better figure out how to build it."

Jim might not be here in the physical, but he still has an influence on me, in the way I manage and protect the brand and build strong relationships.

INTELLECTUAL PROPERTY INFRINGEMENTS

I had to go forward and learn what it all meant on my own. One of the first lessons was that I could go out and create a brand, but it wasn't a sure thing that I owned it. The ® wasn't enough. Registration was just the first step. It only gave you the right to go to court to try to defend your brand, and at your own expense. It boiled down to this how much money do you have to protect this investment?

The attorneys I talked to also said I had to show paper trails of how many times I've defended it. I developed a hawk-eye, looking for anybody who used the brand. I then made sure they received a letter informing them they were using my intellectual property. I have someone full-time now who does nothing but look for brand infringements. Once you've invested in your brand, you have to make sure you also invest in the protection of that brand.

"CELTIC SEA SALT"

There have been a lot of infringements on the Celtic Sea Salt brand. One of the most common still happens online, when people include "Celtic Sea Salt" as a keyword search term for their own websites. So, when people search for "Celtic Sea Salt" online, they will be directed to their website instead. This is an ongoing thing. We have to send letters to five to ten companies a month just to inform people. We now have a full-time person managing infringements. Most of them stop, but the people who are serious figure out loopholes to continue to try to do it. But we've pretty much nipped the big companies, I do believe.

LOGO INFRINGEMENT

We also had an infringement with the logo. Our logo is a picture of a man with a wooden rake in his hands, harvesting salt. We came across a Harris Teeter product that had that same kind of logo. It didn't look the same, but it could be confused for our salt if somebody said, "Could you go to the store and get that salt that has the man raking on it?" That's enough to be an infringement.

So, we sent a letter to Harris Teeter to say "This is our brand. It could cause confusion." And within a week, they sent a beautiful letter back that basically said, "We are so sorry. We are in the process of changing the label right away." They didn't have to do that. But the integrity was there, and that's worth sharing.

The problem with a logo is that when you register it, there's not really a search done for the actual design, but there's a search for the description of the design. So, it's important to be as detailed in the description of the design as possible, just to help protect the brand.

NO PATENTS ON COMMODITIES

For our situation, you must remember that salt is a commodity, and a commodity is accessible to everybody. It's not patented. It's not a special formulated ingredient or anything like Ben's Original rice or Quaker Oats.

Our company had been doing business with New Zealand and Australia for years because of a macrobiotic student who used to buy from Jacques and Yvette before Philippe and I got involved. They continued to buy, even when Philippe and I took over the company. Then they said they wanted to register the brand because they saw we were registering the brand in the United States. We gave them permission to do it, not understanding, really, what that meant.

They registered the brand, and then they changed the ownership of it. The new owner went directly to the suppliers and started buying from them, so that whole distribution channel was completely lost overnight.

But the wonderful thing is that if you watch these brands, even though you might have lost them, people might eventually abandon them too. They might forget to re-register or renew, which is what happened with the brand in New

Zealand and Australia. The people who had it eventually abandoned it. Now we can open distribution channels in those areas again since we do still get a lot of calls from people asking if we are the original Celtic Sea Salt company. We say "Yes, but we can't sell to you because the brand is registered and owned by someone else in New Zealand." Now we've got the registration back. I didn't understand what that meant at the time.

AQUON MATRIX®

When you do have a registration, you have to make sure you have a product in distribution. You can't go out and just register ten brands without putting anything on the market. You have to show proof of the brand actually being sold.

For example, we had another brand called Marine Matrix, which was ocean water that was very bioavailable to assimilate. We couldn't get that product into the United States for some time because of FDA regulations. In that gap in time, we couldn't commerce with that brand, so we had to abandon the name. In the meantime, another company was able to register Marine Matrix. Now they have it. They haven't done anything with it, and they said they were getting it to save it for me. But we haven't done anything with that company.

Anyway, that just goes to show you that somebody else may be watching your brand, just waiting for the minute they can grab it. In the meantime, we have had to rebrand this product to bring it to the U.S. market. Miguel, who used to work for the company we used to source this product from, reached out to me about five years ago to see if I wanted to partner with him to bring this product back to market. This time, it would be even better, with a very convenient to-go packet with 10 cc of filtered seawater structured for better absorption. I am really excited to have this product back to complement our mineral offerings. You can find Aquon Matrix® on our website, and it is recommended by some of the doctors in our database. It is supposed to support mitochondrial defenses because of its availability of minerals for absorption. This has been very helpful for my granddaughter Maya.

18 MONTHS AND $85,000 LATER

One of the biggest infringements that we have ever had was from a huge natural products brand. I knew the owners of this other brand from the macrobiotic community, and we attended the same family potlucks in California. They took the Celtic Sea Salt brand to the Supreme Court to try to get Celtic Sea Salt categorized as a generic term. I thought since it was registered, I could just show the ® and we'd be done. This is when I learned it would not be so easy.

At a trade show, months into the legal suit, I saw the owner of that brand and asked him face-to-face why he was doing this. He smiled and replied, "Because I can." And that was that. It took about 18 months and $85,000 to finalize an agreement that they could use "Celtic Sea Salt" on one of their products, a jar of sea salt. But they couldn't use it in advertising or in any kind of recipes or anything.

I had to finally settle because I didn't have any more money to keep fighting them, and they had a lot left to keep fighting me. Even the attorney said, "I don't know why they're doing this because even if they win, they're never going to make the return from their sales with all these legal costs."

It didn't make sense, but it did open my eyes that I had better really protect this intellectual property. It also opened my eyes that there must be some extreme value to the name if somebody was going to go to such expense to try to get it from me. My biggest lesson from this was if the "Celtic Sea Salt" name falls, then the whole company falls. This also got me thinking about the importance of diversifying into a family of brands instead of just one.

GROWING A FAMILY OF BRANDS

That sounds easier than it has been. So far, we have registered and gone to market with Celtic Light Grey Sea Salt, Celtic Sea Salt, Flower of the Ocean (or fleur de sel), and Makai Pure (an amazing high-alkaline salt). I talked about the last two in the previous chapter. We also have other brands, such as Electrolyve, as well as Rare Body and our Celtic Super Seasoning. So now, if something happened to Celtic Sea Salt, we would still have the Flower of the Ocean, Makai Pure, and so on. I have learned about making sure to expand on your one intellectual property and avoid putting all your eggs in one basket.

Following advice from my mentor Jim, I realized I needed "Celtic Sea Salt" to help introduce the Makai salt, in particular. Otherwise, the customer wouldn't even notice it on the shelf. We started with the Celtic Sea Salt words and logo large, front and center, with "Makai" smaller below it. Once it gained momentum, we did another label edit and made Makai bigger and Celtic Sea Salt smaller while keeping Celtic Sea Salt as the brand. You should have seen our marketing meetings coming up with the copy: "Celtic Sea Salt's Makai Sea Salt." We drove ourselves and each other crazy trying to find a way to communicate one brand with another brand to the customer without sounding like SEO on the back end of a website. We soon came up with a better solution.

SELINA NATURALLY

As we continued to grow the Celtic Sea Salt brand, we realized the name kept us in a box that would not allow us to expand. We wanted to brand other products that did not have anything to do with CSS, so we needed a more neutral and broader name. We decided we needed to create a mother company so we could put a variety of different products underneath that one. Through many hours and with all the employees offering input, we finally came up with "Selina Naturally," which was cute.

Susan Bloom, one of my employees, came in one morning and she said, "I got it. Selina. Naturally. Like, Selina Naturally. It's kind of like, it depends on where you put the accent." Since my name is Selina, which is close to "saline," or salty, it made sense. So, Selina Naturally it was.

Selina Naturally was a broad enough name that we could do almost anything with it. It really helped us get out of the grey box. Jordan Rubin was the founder and owner of Garden of Life, as well as a great friend and mentor. He said, "You should keep it together by saying 'Selina Naturally, the home of Celtic Sea Salt.'" So that's what Selina Naturally is today. The brand brings salts other than Celtic Sea Salt to the marketplace.

PROMOTION AND INFLUENCE

I have a distributor, June Lim, who has a company called Radiant Code in Malaysia. She's a huge macrobiotic distributor with beautiful restaurants and cafés. She also does these amazing health summits in Malaysia for cancer patients and people with chronic illnesses. She invited me to come to one of these to teach about Celtic Sea Salt.

Since I'm completely terrified of speaking in front of people, I hired a coach to help me build and work through the presentation. I really put a lot of investment energy into it.

So, I was at the summit in Malaysia, sitting in the front row with a panel of speakers from all over the world. I was up next, and I was so nervous. The lady next to me was from

Japan, and she was sitting there practically holding my hand. "It's okay," she told me. "It's okay."

Well, the man at the front of the room was from Amsterdam and, little did I know he had one message to convey, and it was not to my benefit. He finished his lecture, then wrote with a marker on the board, "CELTIC SEA SALT," in big letters. Then he put a big line through it, and he said, "Do not eat it. It's bad for you." Then it was time for me to get up and speak. June ran up to the board and she erased it fast. Then she introduced me.

It turned out the man had a salt he wanted June and her foundation to start promoting. He was there to try to get her to promote his salt. That is what is usually at stake when people debate the Celtic Sea Salt brand. It's because they have their own agenda.

At the end of the day, I believed I had manifested that whole thing to happen because that's what fear does to you. I mean, I was scared to death to speak. Then I got up there and the sound system didn't work, so the introduction to the video was silent and I had to improvise. But I'm still here, and they still use our salt. They've expanded their business in Malaysia. So, it all worked out.

But imagine if that man had tarnished the Celtic Sea Salt name with that gesture. That's always the danger. They say a person in Hollywood can one day be the king of the hill and the next day be at the very bottom of it—just from bad news. Your brand is the same thing. The value of a brand is in how well you defend it.

I hope people take away from this chapter the fact that, because of the internet, infringements are a lot easier for people to get away with now because of the keyword search engine. As you register a brand, make sure you also register all your platforms. For example, if you're going to register Celtic Sea Salt, you should get the URL for Celtic Sea Salt, as well as on Facebook, Instagram, Twitter, and so on. It's important to understand there are going to be people who want to capitalize on brands because they're like shortcuts to get market share.

I'll talk more about international expansion in the next chapter on distribution, but when we expand internationally, the international manager fills out a whole bunch of paperwork and sends it to my guy, who really takes care of the brand. He then does a search to see how much it'll cost for us to register the brand in that country. If the brand registration costs thousands of dollars, we have him look to see if we can get the URL in that country. If we can't afford to get the registration for the brand, we will go after the URL.

Today, we have registered the Celtic Sea Salt brand in all the European Union countries. We've registered it in Malaysia, China, Hong Kong, and Canada, and we are now in the process in New Zealand and Australia. We are continuing to expand. We're not going to go out and register the brand in every single country, but as soon as the country shows an interest, we explore how we should protect our intellectual property.

Intellectual property and brand promise is probably the most important thing for people to understand when running a company. It's something that we have done well, in good part because we've gotten influential people to promote the brand. There are some people who promote the Celtic Sea Salt brand, and they'll tell me, "You know what, Selina? I do a lot of health lectures and a lot of seminars, and I really don't promote any brand but Celtic Sea Salt. I almost feel like it's a type of salt."

When a brand is promoted right, it can often feel like that. Marketers work to get it on the tip of everyone's tongue, like Band-Aid or Kleenex. Those are brands we think of as types of things. Instead of sea salt, our influencers think Celtic Sea Salt.

That was really our experience growing the brand and coming to understand the amazing power of a brand in general. In the next chapter, I'll explain how we went about getting the volume and movement so that we could pay to defend it. When we first got involved with Celtic Sea Salt, it was a mail-order business with a few little stores that we then expanded into more than 3,500. In the next chapter, I'll explain how we went from there to getting our salts into major distribution, with brokers and everything. Get ready to see how fast your margins can change overnight after getting into distribution!

7

Distribution and Sourcing

Sometimes adversity is what you need to
face in order to become successful.

—Zig Ziglar

THE FLOOD was really a catalyst for rethinking distribution as well. It forced me to figure out how we were going to keep business going overall. In the same way, I looked at the salt fields in Brittany and thought, "I better diversify with other sources of salt." I now thought, "We should have multiple channels of getting our products to the customers."

To do this, we would need to make some changes. We had the newsletter and a catalog. But about 80 percent of our business was from other people's branded products that we sold through our own outlets, our catalog, and our website. I now wanted to figure out how I could make money with the intellectual property that Jim Cockman had taught me about so well.

Like I mentioned in the previous chapter, our big intellectual properties at the time were Aquon Matrix, Celtic Sea Salt, Light Grey Celtic Sea Salt, and Flower of the Ocean. Those were the big brands that I was really promoting, and they made up most of our revenue stream. Today, we've expanded to other brands, such as Makai Pure® Salt, and we've developed an electrolyte powder, Electrolyve®, and branched out into the bath category with our Rare Body® brand. We're also doing Celtic Super Seasonings™ and Sensible Salts®.

If I wanted to go this path, I would have to build the IP, protect it, and also distribute it. I couldn't take it for granted that business was going to grow without me constantly looking for platforms to get our brand in front of the public. Note that today, with the internet, visibility is a lot different. Back then, we had to continue the momentum of keeping the brand out there through other means.

It is a good thing we developed such a demand for the CSS brand because this was the foundation that would make the next plan work. After the flood, we needed to pivot and expand into wholesale distribution. I had to figure out not just how the company could survive but also how to continue to protect the brand as intellectual property and how to go out there and sell it. That's what distribution is about.

WHOLESALE DISTRIBUTORS

I wrote up a very informal new business plan. We were going to go through a distributor to get our first broker. The distributor would then be selling to stores, such as Whole Foods and Sprouts. We were already successfully selling directly to over 3,500 stores across the United States, and in Canada and Malaysia, but I knew we had the capacity to expand into more.

First, in case you don't know, a distributor is an intermediary with huge warehouses positioned all over the country. A brand ships its pallets of products to the warehouses, and then the stores order from the warehouses. Essentially, the distributor stores the product and does fulfillment. Sometimes they will run ads or deals to the stores and then the stores will pass the deals on to the customer, such as 10 percent off a product.

The distributors really do zero selling. It's the brokers who make sure the products come from the distribution warehouses and get to the retail stores. I'll talk more about brokers in the next section. When you see big trucks going down the highway with UNFI, KeHE, or US Foods, those are distributors.

Some stores, like Publix, don't go through distributors. They order directly because they have big enough warehouses to do it that way. But imagine a buyer for a whole foods store. They would have to contact every single vendor to get all the products on the shelf. But with a distributor, it's a one-stop deal. There's only one check they have to write and one place to contact about everything.

To try to understand how we were going to go into distribution, I started to look at our database to figure out who we could partner with. At this time, we already had Azure Standard on the West Coast and Health Flavors on the East Coast. Now, I didn't get these distributors by being proactive. They came to me because of the brand, or the intellectual property. They realized that it had a good following and a lot of influential people promoting it. But we only had these two little distributors, and they were only servicing the Northeast and the Northwest. Their distribution territory was very limited.

We also had a Canadian distributor, and he was very passionate. He wanted to completely duplicate the entire company, The Grain & Salt Society, with the newsletter and the catalog and everything. But in Canada, they don't have the same kind of distribution platform as in the United States. The demographics are a lot more spread out, so mail order is not that big of a marketing platform.

But we did start a Canadian chapter. We partnered with this guy and his brother for a good two or three years, and we did good business with them. We brought the salt into Canada in bulk, and they repackaged it with labels that were just a little different to be compliant with Canadian requirements.

But then one day, we got a notification from a legal authority in Canada saying that if we did not stop selling to this distributor, we could lose our brand. Canada is strict in how it honors intellectual property. When we investigated further, we discovered that an employee had told the authorities in Canada that the company was ordering the

Celtic Sea Salt from us, but they were also supplementing it with another salt. This went against Canadian law, so we had to stop distribution immediately because of their lack of integrity. It was a great blessing to be notified, but now we were losing $200,000 per year in sales.

There are a lot of different things you must understand to be compliant in another country. For instance, in Canada, you cannot have your products on the store shelves unless the packaging is bilingual. Not only did it take us a long time to get back into Canada, but we had to take our entire line and change all the labels, so they were printed in both French and English. Now we're in Canada again, working with a distributor and doing well.

BROKERS

Before we found a broker, we were selling to Whole Foods and Earth Fare directly. But I could not seem to get into other stores, like Sprouts and Publix. They said they wouldn't talk to a salesperson. We needed a broker because that's how they worked.

That's when I interviewed my first broker, one of the largest brokers on the East Coast. We decided to go ahead and go with them. They charged 2 to 7 percent commission, and we agreed to 5 percent. We were already doing a lot of sales in stores, over $2 million annually, but how this would change was hard for us to digest. The distributor needed at least 25 percent, and the broker would take 5 percent. So, now we would be making 30 percent less than what we were making before selling directly to the retailer.

We also had to do some pricing changes to pay for the shipping to these new distributors. It was a huge learning curve, and we made a lot of mistakes. But my CFO, my sister Theresa, was amazing throughout. We called different people who had businesses and picked their brain to learn from them. At the end of the day, we would figure it out.

Now, Theresa does what we call "mini P&Ls," which are profit and loss calculations for every single distributor. Throughout a profit and loss, we also look at every account the distributor sells to. We can really keep a good eye on what SKUs they're buying, how much we're charging them, and the movement of items—all to make sure we're always making a profit.

What we soon found out was that we weren't just agreeing to the 5 percent to the broker and the 25 percent for the margin for the distributor. When we would place orders, they all had a net 45 days to terms. My sister, the CFO, started getting checks for $10,000 when we were expecting ones for maybe $30,000. She was livid. "How am I supposed to pay the bills? I don't even know what a true sale is and how much money is going to be coming in!"

Thank God she did not have a heart attack because the learning process was a huge struggle. My advice to anybody developing any products today is to make sure you have put all the different margins in there for the intermediaries to make sure you can still afford to go to market. We had a good margin from the beginning, so we were able to survive, but it was very scary.

There were some years we would write off over $100,000 in disputes. This was the amount we could not get back from some of these distributors, and that's a huge chunk of money! We were constantly yelling, "What the heck? I can't believe this! They're not paying us. We have to figure this out!"

As an example of a dispute, we might see that they took $10 per pallet off as a "pallet charge." We didn't understand why or what that meant, so we would have to write up this lengthy letter just to say, "Please help us understand why you took $10 off for every pallet," and also that we were disputing the charge. We had to put all the disputes in writing.

Or they might take $5,000 off as a "slotting fee." A slotting fee is a charge for shelf space. For example, to get into Sprouts, it cost us a $40,000 slotting fee, and they double charged us! For whatever reason, distributors would just take money off from what they owed us, or they'd overcharge us. It could easily take a year to get that money back.

We now have a good relationship with the distributors and brokers and better communication overall. But this changes constantly. As soon as a check comes in with any kind of issue, we have a system in place to submit these disputes quickly. The magic is to get them to respond to the disputes. Now we have a person in sales, Ariane, and my shipping manager Matt is getting some better results in collecting money owed to us.

OTHER CHANNELS

It was the diversification of all the other channels that really helped us get through this. We were already selling on Amazon, iHerb, and Thrive—which are all ecommerce platforms. We also have over 1000 doctors in our database who promoted Celtic Sea Salt and sold it in their practices. We also had our ingredient customers, as well as our international branches.

INTERNATIONAL BRANCHES

In full disclosure, all the international branches were done very reactively, not proactively. After Canada, our next international distributor was June Lim, the owner of Radiant Code in Malaysia. I mentioned her in the last chapter. She contacted me and said she had gone to a seminar with vegan chef Al Chase and he kept talking about how important it was to eat Celtic Sea Salt. Since she already had quite a few cafés, stores, and distribution outlets, she said, "Well, if it's that important, I'm already importing products from all over the world into Malaysia. I might as well bring in Celtic Sea Salt too."

Knowing the importance of intellectual property and protecting it, we went ahead and registered in Malaysia. June used all our copy, as well as our logo, and had the label designed in Malaysia. That's been a very, *very* good distribution channel for us, and it has really expanded.

AMAZON

As the internet expanded, I realized it was important to diversify our online distribution also. Amazon.com was growing, but there were a lot of unknowns at that time. They were new, and we were new to them. We didn't understand how to get the products moving. There were quite a few different ways you could sell on Amazon, and we had a huge learning curve to figure it all out.

We started on Amazon on our own, and then we bought a broker to help us manage it. It's funny because the whole time we had the broker, sales were down, but now sales are exploding because of COVID-19 and because Amazon has become a distribution giant. We are spending about $20,000 per month on Amazon ads. My niece Stephanie is managing the ads and uploads, and Ariane is getting cross-trained on Amazon management.

OTHER ONLINE MARKETPLACES

The other online stores, such as Thrive and iHerb, have grown, too, since COVID-19. But the one that has really expanded us internationally is iHerb because it allows you to shop on the website, and it handles all countries. It's global.

In fact, I was at a seminar in Portugal and there was a man there from Israel. I told him what I did. He said, "Oh, we use Celtic Sea Salt in my house in Israel." I said, "You're kidding." He said, "No, my wife orders it from iHerb." So, you can see that our online diversification has also gone international.

CELEBRITIES

We all know the attention a celebrity can give a brand, so when I had an opportunity to offer our salt at the Oscar and Emmy ceremonies as gifts to celebrities, I took it. I had an idea to create a little tag that went on each shaker jar. The tags offered our services as a gifting hostess at the receiver's next dinner party. If contacted, I would coordinate party favors with our Celtic Sea Salt with notes in each bag thanking the guests for coming to the party.

*Carol Connors (middle) and me (on left) at Spago,
with Wolfgang Puck behind us (on right)*

I was contacted by Carol Connors (pictured above), who cowrote the theme song for *Rocky,* along with many other songs used in major films. I would have never imagined the dear friend Carol has become to my family. She wrote me a song about Dominic and my life with him called "Dignity Through His Eyes." She said the song just came pouring through her.

Carol has connected me and our salt with so many other celebrities, such as her friend, Barbi Benton, a famous retired model and actress. When Carol told her about me, she said, "I have been using Celtic Sea Salt for years," and she pulled some out of her purse in a baggie. Carol said she gets it out and shares it with the audience to put on their popcorn at some of the movie opening previews.

Barbie Benton (on left) and me at the Copper Palace
in Aspen, Colorado, during her birthday party

Right before the airlines shut down for the pandemic, Barbi (pictured above) invited me to her birthday party at the Copper Palace in Aspen, Colorado. I had a gift bag on the table for each guest, and Barbi stood up and told the Celtic Sea Salt story.

HEALTH PROFESSIONALS

When Jacques first started the company, the brand was really grown by Bruce West, William Campbell Douglass, and Sally Fallon, founder of the Weston A. Price Foundation. Jacques even wrote a chapter for Sally's book, *Nourishing Traditions*, about bread and ancient grains. They had large audiences, and they told people that they should eat Celtic Sea Salt. I thought there might be something there because when you think about it, most people make their decisions based on what they're told by a doctor, a spiritual leader, a celebrity, or someone else in an influential role.

I thought I should probably reach out to more doctors aligned with health and nutrition about our salt and the kinds of results people are getting with it. I went to different chiropractor shows to develop relationships, and I offered doctors little gifts for new patients, like free salt. I also presented the nutritional facts of the mineral analyses and testimonials from people who ate the salt. I really just appealed to their common sense.

Some of the doctors even realized the value of having our salt in their offices. A pediatrician in Miami told us that when kids come in not feeling well, he has the nurse give them a warm solution of water with a little bit of Celtic Sea Salt in it. He said 50 percent of them feel well enough to go home after that. Even doctors themselves have started to collect testimonials. Many of the testimonials in this book were provided by David Brownstein, MD.

I remember going to a chiropractor in California one year and when I walked in, I saw Celtic Sea Salt on shelves behind the reception desk. I was in awe. The chiropractor said, "Oh, yeah, every patient who comes in here, the first thing we do is sell them a pound of salt."

Today, we have over 1000 doctors in our database because we've really cultivated those relationships. These days, the revenue stream from our professional branch is not as big as it was because people like the convenience of going to Amazon to get everything. But we really use our doctors to launch new products because, like I said, most people will take a doctor's advice. If a doctor says you should use this, people usually do. We continue to cultivate those relationships and utilize them for new product launches. They are great with it.

I have developed amazing personal relationships with so many of the influential professionals who have awakened us to ways of obtaining optimal health and well-being. I would love to mention all of them in this book, but there was so much I wanted to say, I had to limit my words of appreciation for what they have done in the wellness movement. You can learn more on our website about people like Donna

Gates, author and founder of Body Ecology; Jordan Rubin, author and founder of Garden of Life; Toni Toney, author and founder of EcoDiet; David Wolfe; Lynne August, MD; and John Salley. These are just a few of many. It's these people who have made Celtic Sea Salt in such demand. I will always have so much appreciation for all their exposure. They are in my prayers.

SALT AS AN INGREDIENT

Early on in my relationship with Jim Cockman, he took me to several grocery stores and walked me around. He said, "Now, I want you to tell me how many potential customers you have in this grocery store." It went over my head. I just looked at the people.

He said, "No, go look at the ingredients of all the products on the store shelves and tell me how many of them say 'sea salt.'" I went, "Wow!" It was an aha moment.

Some companies, like Applegate Farms and French Meadow Bakery, were using Celtic Sea Salt as an ingredient, but I hadn't gone after them to promote it. They already wanted a high-quality product with Celtic Sea Salt in it. So, we had some ingredient customers, but I had no clue about the real potential here.

Now, it seems easy to have ingredient customers because they can place an order for a whole pallet of salt, and it just goes out to them. It's very easy packaging. The salt comes in, and it goes out. But there is also a huge responsibility with ingredient customers because they are putting our product, as an ingredient, into the mix with other products. It all becomes a huge investment in the making of their final product.

A HORSE REVIVED BY CELTIC SEA SALT

A few years ago, a woman by the name of Gene Gage, the owner and operator of an equine training and boarding facility for more than 40 years, contacted me from Punta Gorda, Florida. She said, "I have a bunch of horse ranches, and I board horses too. They stay here, and I take care of them." She told me a story.

She said one of her clients had a horse that was so ill, it would not drink or eat. The veterinarian said, "If this horse doesn't have a turnaround within a couple of days, we are out of options." She had some Celtic Sea Salt on her table. She read the label, which stated how the product contains electrolytes that help the body's homeostasis. She was interested, and she wondered what might happen if she put the salt in the horse's water.

She experimented with a tablespoon of salt in the water. Later that day, when she went back out, the water was gone. The horse's eyes looked clear, and the horse looked better overall. She did it again the next day, with the same results.

The woman then called the veterinarian and said, "I need you to come and look at the horse because I can't believe what's going on." The veterinarian came out and checked the horse's vitals and said, "Wow! This is amazing. Whatever you've done is really working." The horse had started to eat again, and its vital signs were healthy and back to normal.

This wasn't the first time I'd heard a story like this. There'd been at least one article written about something similar. Gene said, "Well, I really want to get into this business. How can I be the broker for the equine market? There are over nine million horses in the United States, and I could see one pound of salt for each horse per month." For comparison, it takes a family about six months to go through a pound of salt.

I flew to Florida to meet with her, and we designed the label and the marketing information. We put a new label on the bags and included a scoop. "They all need a scoop," she said. "Because when you're out in the barn, you don't have anything to scoop it out with." There it was: our new line of equine salt. That line has been growing a lot. We just did a huge order with Tractor Supply. I never would have thought we would have gotten into that category.

ADVERSITY

This chapter has focused again on dealing with adversity, on facing challenges, and learning from them to grow the business and succeed. I really think you have to be flexible and fluid to handle adversity. Because if you stay rigid and in fight-or-flight mode, your body is not going to be able to continue for much longer. You may be able to get through the immediate issue, but you won't be able to keep going.

But it wasn't from running the company that I learned about dealing with adversity; it was really from my son. I talked a little about this in a previous chapter, but in the next I will share a lot more about my life with Dominic. It was thanks to him that I learned to ride the waves and surrender and to approach adversity within the business with a calmness and peace of mind as well.

8
Lessons from Dominic

Character cannot be developed in ease and quiet.
Only through experience of trial and suffering
can the soul be strengthened, vision cleared,
ambition inspired, and success achieved.

—Helen Keller

SO FAR in this book, I've shared a number of lessons about business and life in general. But I think I learned the most from a person who never spoke a word: my son, Dominic, who lived to be only 28 years old. Because of my experience with him, I've come to believe that we choose to be here. And also, that our story is written even before we're born. This chapter will tell the story of how I came to this conclusion.

Dominic's body was completely incapable of functions that we take for granted. He never held anything in his hands, and he never stood or walked. After the age of five, he even lost the strength to hold himself up. The adversity

Dominic endured was being in a body that did not do what he wanted it to do.

Dominic also taught me about uncertainty and how to surrender over and over again. As I related in a previous chapter, having a child with needs as special as Dominic's meant I didn't have a "normal" experience as a first-time mother. I couldn't compare my experience to other mothers with children who were already growing and developing: sitting up, starting to crawl, or saying "mama" for the first time. I didn't have any of these milestones that bring joy to most mothers and help balance out all the sleepless nights.

Instead, I was left wondering if my son was ever going to speak, or even if he was ever going to be able to hold anything in his hand. I would be advised to go to support groups with other parents of special needs children, but I didn't like that view of "normal." Their experiences were more similar to mine, but it felt like a big, ongoing pity party. I couldn't let myself give in to that emotion since it would weaken what strength I needed to persevere each day. It also wasn't the path I wanted to take. So, being Dominic's mother meant I had to create my own sense of normalcy. I read a book titled *Happiness Is a Choice*, by Frank Minirth and Paul Meier, and this is the path I wanted to walk.

LEARNING TO SURRENDER

Surrender can have a few meanings. The *surrender* I am referring to is the kind of surrender Michael Singer writes about in his book *The Surrender Experience*. He says it takes courage to surrender because we don't always want to do what is presented to us. That's pretty much everything in life. It's about surrendering your will and letting God's will come forth.

Taking care of Dominic was difficult enough. But how did I get up every day and also run a business while still making sure all my kids had their needs met? It wasn't until I started writing this book that I realized the business was the place where I had some control. My husband used to say, "You're just so absorbed by this company. You don't have a life because you're so into this company." Now, I realize it was my escape, as well as my family's security because Dominic's care required a lot of money.

Running the company also meant dealing with adversity and overcoming obstacles. But with the company, it was very strategic. It was X and Y can equal Z, with a clear cause and effect. With Dominic, it was rarely clear what caused what. Even when I would mess up or something didn't work out very well with the business, I could figure out what I did wrong. A mistake could be fixed. *Well, then, I'll just try something else.*

There's a lot of judgment of anyone running a business, especially a woman, and I was a target for judgment over having Dominic as well, but somehow I handled it with more grace. For example, once at a get-together at a Christian school with my best friend, a woman came up to me and said, "It's because of your lack of faith that Dominic is still in a wheelchair."

I asked myself, "Is that true?" I had thought the very same thing myself at one point. My girlfriend Gloria wanted to punch that woman in the face, but I handled it with a lot more grace than I would have if someone had said, "You should be running the company differently." I've always been really harsh on myself about how I run the business, which is probably why I've never taken criticism about it very well.

I think this is because I could read a book on how to run a business or how to write a business plan. I could call a mentor. There were so many resources I could go to that if I messed up with the business, people would say "Are you stupid? Didn't you read the book? Don't you know Business 101?" With Dominic, there was no rule book, no normal. I was doing my very best, and every day was charting unknown waters.

In Chapter 3, where I told the story of Dominic's birth, I mentioned a nurse who came to me in the hospital and said, "It's all going to be okay." What that meant, I didn't know at the time. Today, I understand that, no matter what you are doing in life, it's going to be okay. We just have to embrace the uncertainty. If we have faith and trust that we are all actually being looked out for—and my belief is God is always watching my back—then it's always going to be okay. It's not going to be easy, but it is going to be okay.

Early on, people urged me to visit some facilities for Dominic, in case something happened to me or if taking care of him became too hard. It had never even entered my mind until then that I would ever, *ever* give my son to someone else. But I eventually went to see a facility, just to have a backup plan in case Philippe or I were not around. I had my niece Sarah in one arm and my son in the other arm. We were walking down the hallway, and in one room there was this little girl with a really, *really* big head. It was her! I had dreamt about this little girl when Dominic was in his coma, during his first ten days of life. I dreamt this so vividly that I recognized the same color bow in her hair. Her eyes looked the same and everything.

The lady giving us the tour saw the shock on my face and asked, "Are you okay?"

Stunned, I said, "I dreamt this little girl. I dreamt all of this." I was trying to figure out how I could have dreamed this. How could I have seen this? Was I psychic? Was it a premonition? I started to question my view of religion then because, being Catholic, you don't believe in things like that.

I didn't know where that was coming from, but it really did happen for me. That's when I started looking at things that were more unknown and that people didn't talk about in the religious community very much. After visiting the facility, my mind was made up against it. There's a kind of love that you need from your family, and I knew he wasn't going to get it there.

There were only two paths that I saw for Dominic at home: the medical approach or a more natural one. I could've taken the medical route and let doctors make all the decisions. "He should be on this seizure medication. If that doesn't work, we'll put him on this. Then this medication to help counter-act the side effects of the first drug." But I thought it just sounded like a big guinea pig experiment. So, I decided to take the natural approach instead and hoped for less intense side effects than the drugs offered.

I fed Dominic the foods that I felt were important for him to thrive at his healthiest potential. In order to do that, I kept a diet diary for him every single day. The diary included every single thing he ate, how long it took him to eat it, how many bowel movements he had (and if the bowel movements were healthy), how many seizures he had, and how he slept. I was trying to find some rhyme or reason for everything I did. I was kind of experimenting, too, I guess, but I felt like the side effects would be fewer than from any medications.

This was the path I took. I'm not saying it was the right path, but since both seemed basically experimental, I went with one that felt best for us. It was not an easy path, and if I had it to do over again, maybe I would choose differ-ently. I really don't know. What I do know is that medical people have said, "I can't believe he lived to be 28 years old! It must've been what you've been feeding him and the way you took care of him." Did my care prolong his life? Again, I really don't know.

I tried all kinds of things to help Dominic, even something called "psychomotor patterning," which focused on growth motor skills. For this treatment, four people would come to the house, and each would move one of his limbs like he was crawling. The thought was that it would help to train part of the brain that was not damaged so that he could actually do physical things. But at the end of the day, it didn't change anything. I even questioned, "Did I give it enough time? Did I give it all that I could've given it?" Now we have learned that this technique is not successful for many children and really just left parents feeling mostly discouraged.

By the time Dominic was ten, I was getting a lot of pressure from his teachers at school saying they really felt he needed to be on antiseizure medication. There were times he would have more than 100 seizures in a day and could barely eat because of them. Finally, I decided to try Depakene under the guidance of his pediatrician. Soon after we started the medication, maybe a week into his daily dosing, he developed hard, black, pebble-like stools, a bloated stomach, and very swollen gums that would bleed.

I tried to stick it out for six months, but seeing Dominic have such intense stomach pains, and with no sign of his seizures being reduced, I decided to stop the medication and look to another remedy. But again, in all the years as his mom, I could not find any rhyme or reason for why his seizures would lessen for a period of time and then increase overnight.

As Dominic continued to grow, we finally broke down and bought a used wheelchair. I would put Carla in my backpack, and my niece Sarah on Dominic's lap, and I would push the wheelchair to the grocery store. We had only one car, and Philippe took it to work since most of his jobs were at least 30 minutes away. So, I would push that wheelchair in the Florida heat with all of these babies and the groceries. I am not saying any of this to make it sound like I'm some kind of warrior. I'm saying it because, as a mother, you do what you have to do. That was my normal, and I'd be so proud of myself once I made it to the grocery store and back. I would unload the wheelchair in the living room and break down in a sort of celebratory cry. "I did it! We made it home, and nobody died. We're all still here!" Looking back, I chuckle at this memory and in disbelief that I actually lived it. It seems like a lifetime ago. That was how the surrendering worked, the kind of faith that I practiced.

Going through all of these things, I think Dominic came close to death so many times in his life. One time, in particular, Dominic did not urinate for days. His diaper remained dry, and we couldn't figure it out. Then he started to turn yellow and his stomach was huge, like a bowling ball was inside it.

For some reason, I still had so much faith in Jacques and Yvette—more than medical doctors. I called Jacques and explained what was going on. I said, "I'm going to take him to the emergency room now." He said, "Okay, that's probably a really good decision, but before you do, let's just try this one technique. Then I would recommend you going ahead and taking him." I had to wait for Philippe to come home anyway because I had Sarah and Carla with me, so I had time.

Jacques said to get some ice water and some really hot water. Then I would get a cloth and dip it in the ice water, then touch the tip of his penis. Then I'd dip it in the hot water and touch the tip of his penis. I did this, alternating between hot and cold for probably 25 to 30 minutes, but it just wasn't working.

However, while I was getting the kids ready to go to the hospital, all of a sudden the urine came out. His stomach went down flat, his color came back perfectly, and it was like, hallelujah, it worked!

It's important to me to share these kinds of stories because Jacques was a very unique person. He had so much research knowledge under his belt with these strange reme-dies. Not all of them worked, but this one really did! Most of them did overall. There was something inside me, and inside Jacques, too, that encouraged taking the natural path.

I couldn't believe it when my sister-in-law, Cynthia, was diagnosed with cancer at age 42. I somehow thought healthy eating would protect us from any disease. She stuck to the natural route, even for treatment, and went to a place called Genesis West in Mexico. Philippe and I flew there to see her while my sister and my mom took care of our kids. While we were there, Cynthia said, "I haven't seen my kids in six weeks, and I don't think I'm getting any better. I really want to see them. I need to get home." I said, "Well, let's figure this out, then."

It turned out that Jacques and Yvette had a motor home we could put her in, since flying was too much for her in her condition and too complicated with her catheter and GI tube. On the drive from Mexico to Northern California, I helped Cynthia take her special herbs. We would grind them up and put them in with food. I told her this was how I gave Dominic his vitamins and stuff too.

She said, "Please stop doing this to Dominic. I'm going to talk for him. He can't tell you what you're doing by making him eat these things that are just horrible. They gag you. Don't do it anymore." I agreed. And then she said, "Always remember if I do cross over first, I'm going to be there for him. Don't be afraid that he's going to be crossing over alone."

I stayed by Cynthia's side for as long as I could, although after weeks of being in California, I needed to go home to be with my kids. Cynthia died shortly after I left. It felt so tragic to have an angel like her leave at such a young age. I can only imagine how Jacques and Yvette felt losing her to cancer since they had helped so many others heal from cancer completely.

What I will always remember about this trip is how Cynthia gave Dominic a voice, and she gave me peace of mind when she said she would be there to receive him in the crossing over. It did feel good to know that. Meanwhile, I had no idea when Dominic would cross over—if it might be soon or still years away. He'd already had so many near-death episodes, like I've said.

One time he cried for three months nonstop. We didn't know what was wrong. Doctors didn't know what was wrong. It was a living hell. I had been working closely with Dominic's pediatrician during this time, and he was a doctor I finally began to trust. He ran some blood work that came back showing Dominic needed a blood transfusion. Without a blood transfusion, he would not live. We moved forward immediately with the transfusion, and Dominic finally had relief.

Once Dominic was about 15 years old, his body started to become seriously uncomfortable. With cerebral palsy, there are tight tendons and tight muscles and loose muscles, and the tight tendons curl everything up. His legs became so curled, it became hard to extend them enough to wash behind his knees.

The physical therapist at school had been saying Dominic needed hamstring extension surgery, and I would say "No, he doesn't. I'm going to keep doing these massages and acupuncture and essential oils and he won't need it." Eventually, I had to surrender and get him the hamstring extension.

While he was recovering, I kept telling the doctor, "You've got to get these casts off because, every time he has a seizure, I think that it's very painful for him because he's curling up." When we took the casts off, there were blood marks on his ankles and the top of his feet where he had been pushing on the casts so hard during his seizures. But the procedure worked overall, and Dominic's legs were a lot more comfortable afterward.

There were many moments with my son when we laughed and enjoyed his kind spirit. No matter with what class, caretaker, or person who worked in the field of special needs children, Dominic was always a favorite. He was very quiet most of the time, but in his silence there was a sweet nature everyone recognized. He had deep dark brown eyes with long, full eyelashes that danced when he blinked or looked around when he observed new spaces.

He spent a lot of time in his recliner in the living room after he lost the ability to hold himself up. The girls and I would be busy in the kitchen, working on homework or just talking about our day, when out of nowhere Dominic would gasp for air and let out a huge laugh. He would always be looking up into the sky or high at a space in the room as if entertained by something we couldn't see or hear. We would all stop and laugh and enjoy the sound of his deep belly laugh at whatever had seemed to tickle him. It was music to my ears to think my son did have some joy in this life, even if I couldn't see who or what made him laugh.

When he was really little, he would use his spit to blow bubbles and giggle like a little baby. His brain never developed past that of a three-month-old, so many of his mannerisms and things he was amused by were at the level of a baby. Sometimes at night, he would dream and burst out laughing so hard, he had to gasp for air.

While the move from Florida to Paradise, California, was hardly easy, we were lucky to find Rita. Rita was Dominic's first real caretaker. She had two sets of boy twins, five kids in total, and raised them all. When she would read to Dominic, she would put her hand on the page and, in her eyes, it seemed to her that he actually wanted to turn the page when she finished. She told me, "I think he knows how to read."

Rita saw Dominic in a new light. In her eyes, I could see she felt hopeful, which was refreshing for me as his mom. It was like Rita had a belief about him that nobody but my mother had ever had. She would take him for walks, and when a bird would chirp, he would look over at it. Then she would say "Look at the dog," and he would look over at the dog. She'd tell me, "He responded to me telling him to look at the dog." She had this beautiful hope that gave him dignity. Rita, for the first time, gave me a taste of freedom, but also while knowing Dominic was with somebody who enjoyed his company and taking care of him.

When we left California, Rita was the hardest one to say goodbye to, but our new family chapter started when we moved to Asheville, North Carolina. Dominic turned 18 years old soon after the move, and I had to go to the courthouse to become a legal guardian to my son, which was really a strange experience. I never thought I would need guardianship over my adult child. An elderly parent, maybe, but for my child it was an odd feeling.

When Dominic was about 20 years old, his spine was curling up so badly that his ribs were starting to compress different organs in his body. So, I surrendered to another required surgery.

It was a pretty intense surgery that required being under anesthesia for 18 hours, so the doctor and I had a conversation about resuscitation. By this point in his life, Dominic was beyond uncomfortable. He would inhale deeply, sounding like he was struggling to get all the air he needed. I guess it was because the curve of his spine caused his ribs to put too much pressure on his lungs. His skin was so thin that bones were almost wearing through in areas, and I feared it would tear with the wrong friction or if he bumped into something hard. Seeing my son's body deteriorate was worse than seeing him die. Given his condition, both his doctors and I knew that things would only get worse, no matter what we did. Treatment only delayed his inevitable downhill progression. Considering the daily torture I watched my son live through, I said, "I am voting to not resuscitate."

But the doctor said, "Well, that's not an option for me because I'm a doctor and I vowed to keep people alive."

I felt so judged because I had to actually voice that I would rather my son not be here than be in the life he had been living. To be judged for making that decision was not easy, even though it felt like the more compassionate choice for my son. The doctor even said, "I'm not going to do this surgery and say that I will not resuscitate him. I won't do it."

After reflecting on our options and seeing how badly he needed this surgery, I made the decision to go ahead with the doctor's stipulations. I said, "Resuscitate him if you have to."

The surgery was successful, but Dominic's recovery was long and painful. His spine was now perfectly straight, with no bend, but we had to carry him around in a cast for over three months. He would urinate in it, and it stank. It was awful. But we survived it. They took the cast off, and Dominic's spine was permanently straight with two steel rods supporting it.

When you pick a child up, they usually kind of curl into your arms, but now it was like picking up a straight board with floppy legs. It became even harder to physically take care of Dominic, but he was definitely more comfortable.

DOMINIC'S ATTRACTION

I think of *attraction* as a reflection of two souls meant to do something together in this lifetime, and maybe in future lifetimes. Dominic had a way of attracting the right people who would benefit from him as much as he benefited from them, like Rita. Irisha was another of these people.

When we found Irisha, I completely fell in love with her. She was a Ukrainian woman raised in Brazil who spoke her mind. She was very straightforward when she would say things to me about Dominic's care. Because my family could see how hard it was for me to hear some of her opinions, they didn't like her anywhere near as much as I did.

Irisha was a very unique being. I was raised Catholic and then became born-again Christian, so I was very religious at the time. She believed in God but also in spiritual things, like energies and reiki. I felt like God had been directing me to more of this way of looking at life. Books and people kept coming into my life through the newsletter and friends. My upbringing gave me one way to look at life and our human existence, but my life became an evolution of experiences and people who have opened and expanded my thinking to finally be in my element. Your reality starts in your mind, just like God's creation started with a thought, which He then spoke into manifestation.

Because Dominic couldn't speak a word, Irisha brought a pretty significant element into our family. She provided another means of communicating, or receiving, how Dominic was feeling. The only other person I felt did this was my mom. She would spend time holding him and reading to him. My mom's interpretation of Dominic would be things like the following. She would take care of him all day for me, and when I came home, he would go into a seizure after not having had any all day. My mother would say to me, "You know, I think he is doing that to get your attention." Even though I would never want him to have a seizure, a part of me felt good that he had some sort of response to my presence. It was like a recognition that I am his Mom. I feel my mom really did have a way of reading him. She just interpreted his responses differently than Irisha.

It was an interesting experience for me because I can only imagine that if Dominic had been normal and if he had found a girlfriend or gotten married, this might have been what it would be like. I would always keep this in mind, that Irisha was like a daughter-in-law, thinking that she knows him better than I do. But at the end of the day, I think Irisha saw I had been at the end of my rope for a while, just trying to figure out creative ways to make his life better. That's what she was all about too: how can I make his life better? She taught me about energy and emotions and how mine could affect Dominic. He was very sensitive to energy, she would say.

I'd been doing his diet journaling all these years to see how food affected his seizures, but now she was teaching me it wasn't just food triggering them; it was also energy and vibration. I went, "Oh shit. Now I have to be careful about how I think as well as what I do. I can't win with this little guy. He's like a barometer of my emotions."

He really was. If I was having a bad day, he would have a bad day. Before, I'd seen it like if he had a bad day, then I would have a bad day. But now I could see that he was also reacting to me. I didn't realize that until Irisha brought it to my attention.

By the time Dominic was 21, Irisha was taking care of him Monday through Friday at her house in Hot Springs, a little over an hour away. I would pick him up every Friday and then drop him back off every Sunday. Every time we made the exchange, she would say something like, "When you dropped him off on Sunday, I noticed he was like this. You must have done this and this or he wouldn't have been like that." I remember dealing with the guilt over what she had said to me, just trying to process the information. I knew she was only saying these things because she loved him.

But sometimes Irisha would say these things in front of my employees, and they were shocked. "How can you listen to that?" It was a hard place. It really was. But she felt she was Dominic's voice. She was speaking for him.

I had learned in my version of "normal" to not judge things like this. I listened and took everything with a grain of salt. I would ask myself, "Is there something I actually can learn from this? Is there something I am doing that I could stop doing to possibly help his life?"

As Dominic continued to grow, his body continued to deteriorate. Every day, I would ask God, "What am I supposed to do?" I didn't think I could do this anymore. I would pray, "God, give me a sign. What does Dominic want me to do? I'm really running out of ideas, and I don't know if I'm making the right decisions anymore."

Physically, we become strong under the weight of pressure. If strength is to be earned, the tearing of muscles to rebuild stronger ones is necessary. Yet, in life we often fear adversity and go to great lengths to avoid it, even though, spiritually, we know we grow the most through trials and testing, which God prepares for us in advance.

A MESSAGE FROM BEYOND

One day I received a call from Elizabeth, a previous employee I hadn't seen in a couple of years. She'd been to see a psychic. She said, "I just had the strangest experience." Neither of us believed in psychics, but she went on to explain that her mother had been diagnosed with cancer and she needed some insight. She told me the psychic was a lady, Joanna Ray, whom we had met a year earlier at a Christian business group.

"I just want to let you know," Elizabeth said, "that I went to go see her and she said, 'Something keeps coming up. I'm hearing a voice. It's not with you, but it's somebody you know, and they're trying to get through. I don't know who it is. I don't know anything, but you might.'"

Elizabeth said at the time she thought of Dominic and of me. Then she had thought, "It's a shot in the dark, but I'm going to call Selina and tell her."

So, I called Joanna Ray and I left a message about making an appointment. When she called me back, she said, "In the time that you left that message, a very strong voice kept coming through, saying that I need to talk to you. There are a lot of messages—28 years of messages."

I said, "28 years of messages is what you're getting?"

"Yeah, 28 years of messages."

"My son's 28 years old."

When I went to see her, I was unsure what to expect. I said, "This is new to me. What do you do? What am I supposed to do?"

"You don't really do anything. I surrender and you surrender and then we'll see what God wants to reveal to me. I will close my eyes, and I usually see a big white screen in front of me, and then I start to see images. Then I start to hear words, and I will come back and tell you different things that I hear. That's how it's going to work." She also told me she'd record the entire thing because I was probably not going to remember any of it.

We got started. First, she said, "I see a woman. I see you. I see a lot of women around you and I see crystals, too, but they have flavor."

I told her that I was in the salt business, and she said that maybe that's what the crystals were.

Next, she said, "I see you as a very strong and power-ful woman, and as an empowerment to a lot of women. You're not a leader or above them. You're in the same realm, all together. I see the crystal bringing a lot of amazing women to you."

I said, "Okay, that's great."

"Now, I'm going to go back and ask about other messages."

I said, "Mainly, I just want to know about my son. Can you ask my son anything? Can he communicate with you? Because he doesn't talk. Can I ask you questions and maybe you can hear him, and you can tell me what he's saying?"

"Let me try." Joanna Ray closed her eyes. When she came back, she said, "I see the two of you as two souls getting ready to come into the physical realm. Your souls are having a conversation about getting to come back into this world and into this life. One of you could have a special need, and the other one's going to be the caregiver because there's going to be a huge lesson that needs to be learned." Joanna Ray said that Dominic raised his hand and volunteered. "I'll be the special needs person."

Then she said I raised my hand and said, "I'll be the person who takes care of him." As soon as she said that, it was as if I was watching a movie. I remembered having this agreement with Dominic and, suddenly, the guilt of giving birth to him at home went away in those few seconds. It was an amaz-ing relief.

Then she said, "Dominic said to me, 'I came here and, even if you would have had me at the hospital, I would have come here with the same condition because we agreed to have this path in our life.'"

It made so much sense. Whether this was BS or it was true, it felt good to me at the time. It was something I really wanted to embrace, so I did. She said, "He's telling you, 'Now that you remember everything, Mom, now it's over. This is what I was hanging in here for. I didn't want to leave until you remembered that we agreed to do this. This was not a mistake. This was not something you did to me. This was nobody's blame. It was the agreement that you and I decided.'"

CROSSING OVER

When I went to work the next day, I told one of my employees, Susan Bloom, the story. She said, "Oh my gosh, I'm going to book a meeting with this lady. She sounds amazing."

I agreed, but I felt really weird. Everything felt so surreal and strange. I was supposed to pick Dominic up later, but I called Irisha and asked her to keep him for another day so I could go out with friends that Friday night.

"Sure, no problem," she said.

I woke up Saturday morning with an unshakable feeling that Dominic was going to die that day. The thought just kept coming: *Dominic is going to die today.* I didn't have any sadness or fear. Just *Dominic is going to die today.* I called Irisha. "How's Dominic doing?"

She said, "He's fine."

I said, "He's going to die today."

"What are you talking about?"

"He's going to die today. I don't know why I'm saying this, but he's going to die today."

I called Carla at her apartment, and I said, "Dominic is going to die."

"What's wrong, Mom? Do you want me to come to the hospital?"

I said, "No, he's not at the hospital, but he's going to die today. Do you want to come to Irisha's with me?"

"No." I don't think she believed me. "Just call me when you get there, okay?"

I stopped at the health food store first. The lady checking me out tried to make conversation: "What are you doing today?" I said, "Well, Dominic is going to die today."

She said, "Oh, are you turning the machines off or something?" I said, "No, but he's going to die today." I felt compelled to keep saying it, I guess because I needed witnesses to this strange feeling I was having.

Then, Irisha called and asked me to stop to get some food for her dogs on my way over. When I picked up the dog food, I noticed a place selling crystals. Joanna Ray had told me to get crystals because she helps a lot of people in comas. Crystals hold energy, and sometimes if you hold a crystal in your hand, it can help someone cross over. I thought, "What the heck."

I went into a place to buy some crystals without knowing anything about any of this woo-woo stuff. I told the guy, "I need crystals. My son is going to die today, and I want him to hold these crystals in his hand."

He said, "By coincidence, the lady that supplies our crystals is right behind you." She was busy stocking the crystals when I turned around.

I said, "I don't know anything about crystals. Can you help me? My son is going to die."

"Oh, I see him." She said he had three angels around him and his breathing was becoming shallow.

As soon as she said that, my phone rang. It was Irisha. "Dominic is breathing really weird right now," she said.

I said, "Okay, I'll be there very soon."

The woman helped me get the crystals. As I was checking out, the guy was booking tickets to see a Hollywood psychic named John Edward, and I said, "I'll buy a couple of tickets because by then, I'm sure my son will have passed away."

He said, "Wow, how do you know this?" I said, "I just know."

He held up a necklace with a little purple angel. "Will you put this on your son, around his neck?" I said sure. I bought two tickets to go see John Edward, the crystals, and my little necklace. Then I drove to Irisha's.

As soon as I walked in, Irisha began talking to me, but it was like one of those Charlie Brown movies where you just hear "blah, blah, blah."

I could smell Cynthia. Cynthia had worn a colostomy bag on her side, so she had a certain smell. I thought, "That's Cynthia. I bet she's here for Dominic. She promised me she would be with him when he crossed over."

I walked into the living room, where Dominic was lying on the couch. He looked up at me as a tear slid down his cheek, and I said, "Dominic, I remember." By then, his breathing sounded almost like something was over his head. He couldn't get air. I asked Irisha for a minute alone with him.

I said, "Dominic, it's okay. I remember that you and I came here for this whole reason. I'm so sorry it took me so long to remember this. It's time for you to go now." I laid him on my chest, and I put the crystals on the windowsill next to me. I had one for each of his family members.

I said, "I'm going to put these crystals in your hand, one for each of your sisters, one for your dad, your grandparents, and your aunts. I'll give these crystals to them, Dominic, after you cross over." So, as the music Irisha put on was playing, I put each crystal into his hand. When I put the very last one in his hand, the music stopped and all of a sudden his head went back and his mouth hung open. His eyes stared straight into the air. Dominic was no longer in his body.

"Is this it? Is this really it? Are you gone?" When I started to lift him up, I kissed his lips and there was no air or anything. He went kind of cold that fast. Then I couldn't get him off of me fast enough. It wasn't Dominic anymore. It was just a body. I didn't know what to do.

This photo was taken a year before Dominic crossed over. We took a nap together and little did I know we would be right next to the window where I would lay out his crystals and hold him during his last few moments alive. I loved holding him in this position because it was the closest I came to feeling like he was cuddling me the way I hoped my first child would. I'm grateful for my friend who took this picture so that I have this precious memory captured.

Finally, something told me to go and get a piece of paper and start writing. What came out was a letter from him, the letter I needed to forgive myself. *I know you did your very best, Mom. I was here for 28 years, and I couldn't do anything for myself but just be. I was telling you, Mama, that's what I want you to do is surrender and just be.* To this day, I'm still learning that: just be. Our experience together is my profound reminder to just be.

In fact, the title of this book was almost *Just Be*. This phrase has since become a constant refrain in my life, from meeting a woman at a conference with a business called Just Be to my personal run-ins with honeybees. In our family, we like to think that the bees are Dominic looking over us.

Months after Dominic crossed over, I went to a two-day Hay House conference that provided spiritual lectures by several speakers. On the first day of the conference, I walked to a restaurant a couple of blocks away during the lunch break. I was practically the only one in the place. Then I noticed two ladies looking at me from across the dining area.

One of the ladies got up from her chair and approached me. She looked as though she was rehearsing something or talking to someone. She said, "Sorry to bother you. I see you are attending the conference by the badge you are wearing."

I said, "Yes, I am. It's great."

Then she said, "I am relatively new to this, but I get messages from beyond, and I think your son wants me to come and tell you something." She said he told her to tell me that he was wearing a red sweater when he crossed. This got my full attention. She told me he said that would let me know it's real. It seemed like it went so fast, and I was left in a daze. She did say Dominic related that I would experience some health problems related to my thyroid, but it would not be chronic and he didn't want me to be fearful.

I told the woman I would like to keep in touch. I asked for her phone number and gave her mine. I went back to the conference and kept thinking about her words. Was it true? I really wished I had been with someone so they could have witnessed it too.

The next day, everyone was leaving after the last speaker, and the two ladies were standing at the door waiting for me. The lady who had relayed the message for me handed me a small jewelry box. I was surprised, but I opened it, and it took my breath away. It was a bracelet with a bumblebee. The reason this took my breath away was because when Dominic took his last breath, this is what I kept hearing: "Just be." I had even started attracting bumblebee experiences. A note in the box said, "Mom, I love you. You are my queen bee."

I was so stunned. She said she went to a jewelry shop nearby because Dominic kept asking her to come and look at something. He told her he wanted me to have that brace-let, and she bought it for me. I've included a photo, on the next page, of the bracelet along with a picture of Dominic that I carried around in my wallet. For some reason, I felt a need to take a picture of this bracelet one day. I am so glad I did, because the day after I took it, I was at a hotel and it must have slipped off the nightstand or something because I left it there.

I called the hotel to see if they had found it, but they hadn't. Thankfully, I have the picture as a reminder of this unbelievable experience.

My bracelet and a photo of Dominic

If I could talk to my 20-year-old self, I would say "Enjoy your son in this moment. Stop trying to fix him, and find a way to see him beyond his physical issues. He is perfect. Find joy in today. And just be."

CONCLUSION

Every human contact is a source of personal enrichment.

—Lawrence Appley,
from *The Power of Positive Action*

MY CURIOSITY has always caused me to question things, and I'm just as curious now as when I was first introduced to sea salt over 40 years ago. If it hadn't been invented by now, I would be the first in line to try to figure out how to make it happen. Like I've shared in the book, I've had a lot of challenges along the way, and I'm sure there are going to be even more. The beauty of it all is I'm still here. I'm still alive. I'm actually in a pretty nice element of my life today.

When I speak about salt or my experiences with Dominic, I realize I now have a certain expertise, yet at the same time, I also know I'm being humbled to always continue to learn. Jacques, my father-in-law, was the same way. I think I have some of that character from my actual father, who was a business person. Maybe all along, being an entrepreneur was in my blood.

I really appreciate the opportunity to be able to do more research and share it with so many people who are interested in learning about the role food plays in their health. What I hope you will take away from this book is the simple understanding that ocean water, sea salt, and our body fluids are so similar in the proportions of their elements (sodium, chloride, potassium, magnesium, sulfur, and calcium), and also their alkalinity, their pH. I hope you can really appreciate that.

Again, I believe that everything is created exactly as it's needed, so we should be eating salt in its whole form. When you find yourself shopping for salt, look for how many minerals are actually in it.

MY INTENTION

My intention in writing this book was really to share my journey of taking a commodity and turning it into a well-known brand all over the world. I explained how we went from mail order to other different methods of distribution, diverse sourcing, and so on. I hope my stories of how I did that will inspire others who may be building businesses.

I'm also hoping people will walk away from this book with the understanding that we're all connected, and every experience we have could lead to finishing something that has been put on the back burner for years. For me, that was meeting someone in Portugal who introduced me to my publishing company. All of our experiences are connected, and we can't ignore them. We have to be open to listening to all of them.

THE IMPORTANCE OF STORIES

I am who I am today and have made it through all of the challenges I have faced with the help of other people's stories on YouTube, at seminars, in newsletters, and, of course, in other books. All these stories have inspired me to say, "If they can do it, I can do it." This is what I hope you take from my story too.

There is a certain magic that happens with an attitude of surrender. When you surrender to uncertainty, rather than fight against it, the outcome will more likely lead to what you really want: to be happy, healthy, and generous. My intention is always to be a portal of God's resources.

I remember always telling stories in my childhood and making sure I knew the moral of any story I heard. "So, the moral of the story is to be kind." That's what I really appreciated. Now, putting my own story into print, I hope similar lessons come across, whether it's to surrender, trust, or be more adaptable.

IN COLLABORATION WITH A HIGHER POWER

Whether you believe in God or some other higher power, I want to share my belief that we are always collaborating in our prayers and meditation with a power that is bigger than ourselves. I hope my words can be that same inspiration for you to understand that in collaborating, in your meditation, or in prayer, you're going to bring in powers you never even knew you had.

I love being able to share the stories of all the different salt sources, and how when I put the intention out that I needed to have salts from all over the world, how all these salts came to me. All the new salts we have in our line of Celtic Sea Salt were brought to me by some divine source. However, I did all the due diligence to research each one of these salts and to bring them in as a complementary line to the original grey salt. Now we feel very confident we can keep up with the demand and make sure the quality Jacques insisted on at the very beginning is going to be continued. Our Celtic Sea Salt brand means integrity.

DOMINIC

As you now know, one of the most amazing experiences of my life was having the honor of being the parent of a special needs child. Dominic never spoke a word, but he was my greatest teacher. If you have the opportunity to be in the life of anyone who has any kind of special needs, don't take them for granted. Make an effort to see the world through their eyes. It makes you appreciate everything you can do and is really a blessing.

I hope this book will inspire anyone with a special needs person in their life to focus not on what they can't do but on what they are doing. For Dominic, this was just being. This is what I think we all need to learn every day of our lives: how to just be. In parenting, especially, we often think we are going to have a child and we're going to control them into being exactly what we want them to be. But that is the biggest joke. All we are doing is giving these children a portal to come through into the physical, and it's up to us to just be their support.

Dominic, Carla, and Colette each came here to walk the paths they were meant to walk, and I've just been here to hold their hands and do my very best to support them. It isn't about creating someone; that's not what it's about. It's about surrendering, allowing, and trusting that you're going to be a good example. But you're not creating anything. They've come here as their own creation.

THE COMPANY TODAY

More recently, I've been going through all of Jacques' old file cabinets. There are four or five of them, and one of my employees, Ian, is helping me. Jacques was a living museum and also such a forward thinker that he was ahead of his time, researching topics that are trending news today. He didn't leave any stones unturned, and his files are an example of this.

The files are filled with letters of testimonials from CSS users, which still keep coming in! They also include information from researchers pioneering alternative health methods and traditional healing, as well as research from the past, including a book from the 1800s and documents dating back to 1746. There are hundreds of topics he had studied and researched. Jacques was a real visionary, and I hope to continue his innovation and further what he intended with the company.

While we already know that sea salt is pretty amazing, we've also come to realize that there are so many other land and sea nutritional properties out there in the form of herbs and mushrooms, for example. So, we are currently enhancing our product line with a new seasoning base with ingredients like rose hips, seven different medical mushrooms, and Moringa (sourced from Jacques' granddaughter Stephanie's company, MOR). We have some really amazing, potent plants and seaweeds—one seasoning has four different kinds of seaweed and contains lots of iodine. We're very excited to bring it to market as our Sea and Land Nutrition.

Lynne August, MD, who has been writing about us for 40 years, has asked us more recently to bring to the market an electrolyte liquid she has developed. She deals with a lot of elderly people who have a lot of mineral deficiencies, and this liquid can be put into water to help with those. So, we're very excited to be bringing products to market that can help our trusted customers build their immune systems.

We also have our new potassium salt, our new single-serve electrolyte packets called Aquon Matrix, and a new electrolyte powder with zinc and cranberry to support the urinary tract and the immune system.

CONTACT AND SOCIAL MEDIA

To find out more about our company, you can go to our social media platforms, Facebook and Instagram, at **www.CelticSeaSalt.com**. You can also go to our website, **www.SelinaNaturally.com**.

On the website, you can get *The Sea Salt Cookbook,* written by my daughter Carla. You can also read more about all the different salt sources and about the influential people who have built this brand.

Finally, you can see the analyses of our salts that I mentioned in the book. We spent a lot of money to reveal a breakdown of the 72-element analysis of each salt that we carry. So, go to the website and have a look!

We also have a customer service line staffed by people who are amazingly educated on sea salt and how important it is. Dial 1-800-TOP-SALT. Feel free to give us a call with any questions.

I also wrote this book with inspiration from all those I've heard talk about similar things. I would love to be able to talk to other audiences and groups of people about my journey and be a support to them the way others have been a support to me. To contact me about speaking, call 1-800-TOP-SALT (1-800-867-7258), email info@selinanaturally.com, or go to **www.SelinaNaturally.com** for contact information.

Writing this book has made me realize that the most essential elements of my life include the love of my family, my love for life, and the support of all of these amazing people in it. On the next few pages, I will end with some final words of appreciation.

GRATITUDE PAGES

Gratefulness is the key to a happy life that we hold in our hands, because if we are not grateful, then no matter how much we have, we will not be happy—because we will always want to have something else or something more.

—David Steindl-Rast

MY GRATITUDE GOES to God, my co-creator in all the elements of my life from the very beginning. I was my mother's first child to live after two full-term stillborn babies. I would also like to thank my mom for giving me a foundation of forgiveness and love and, as I spend more time with her, I am even more grateful that she was able to raise all five of her children with such grace. I am grateful for my stepdad "Popi" for taking on a family of five children and being there for me.

Of all the elements of my life, my family is the main one. Having these people in my life has been everything, and I feel so lucky to have been born into such a loving family. I am so grateful for all of them, especially my sister Teece, my CFO and partner in business; she is always watching my back.

A photo of our family! From the left, my sister, myself, our mother, my brother, and my other two sisters.

I would also like to thank my daughters, Carla and Colette, for their unconditional love and friendship. I am so thankful for the sacrifices they made for their brother, Dominic, and the company while growing up. My daughters are my best friends.

Carla came with a zest for cooking foods that support well-being and is always here when I need her to help me figure out remedies in my personal or business life. Carla also has skills in writing and sat with me for hours while I tried to complete this book. She helped me work through the emotions that surfaced so I could share my stories with authentic intentions and clearly get my points across. She also wrote a recipe book that shares a timeline of her grandfather and the company that you can now find on our website: **www. selinanaturally.com**.

My daughter Colette has complemented my life with her go-getter strength, and she makes me feel better just by being around her energy. When I need advice, she always has the right words. She opened Rare Body Studio, her Pilates business, in New York City about a year before the pandemic hit and then relocated it to St. Petersburg, Florida. Her tenacity to make things like this move happen reminds me of myself. She is a manifester in her community. She now has a waiting list for her classes, and she is organizing fitness parties for kids.

My niece Stephanie, my sister Teece, my daughter Carla (with child), me, my niece Sassy, and my daughter Colette

I am grateful for my two grandchildren: Maya, 7, and Kai, 1. Maya loves to tell stories, and her illustrations are remarkable. I crave spending time with both of them. I am still getting to know Kai, but currently she loves to put her head on me and hum. Maya also has seizures, which means that Carla is experiencing the same challenges I did of trying to manage and control her daughter's health issues through nutrition. Currently, Maya is doing well, and Carla and George are making the best of this journey as parents. Maya and Kai are pictured below.

Maya

Kai

I am grateful to my son, Dominic, for helping me see beyond the physical. In his wordless existence, he taught me how to surrender, how to be empathetic and compassionate, and, most importantly, how to love unconditionally.

I am grateful for my niece Sarah, whose zest for life spoiled my pity parties. She helped me get through those first years of Dominic's life. She now has three sons: Bryce, Brayden, and Alex. Bryce and Brayden spend their summers with me, just like Sarah used to.

I am grateful for my dad and stepmom for loaning me the money to acquire the company. My dad's messages telling me that he is praying for me and how proud he is of me are invaluable.

I am grateful for my best friend, Jon, for holding a space for me, and for always being there for me and my girls after Philippe and I separated.

I am grateful for having met someone in Portugal who introduced me to this publishing company with the skills to keep my words authentic and real that was able to hold my hand as I told my stories.

I am grateful to my ex-husband, Philippe, for the journey we had together that helped me to become the person I am today. He gave me a glimpse of a lifestyle that absolutely changed me. I was always so amazed by his skills and the innovation with which he provided for our family, even when we didn't have any money. For example, he created a custom wheelchair for Dominic and a device so we could take him for bike rides.

I am grateful to my in-laws, Jacques and Yvette, for being the pioneers they were and paving the road to change for the better.

I am grateful for my niece Stephanie, Cynthia's daughter, for being such an important part of the company and my life. Stephanie has been blessed with a beautiful son and daughter, Tya and Serigne. I don't get to see them as much as I'd like to since they live in Senegal.

Tya

Serigne

I am grateful to my staff for our shared dedication to supplying this essential commodity of whole sea salt.

I am grateful for all my customers. I bless them every morning in my prayers.

I am grateful for my salt suppliers.

I am grateful for all the influential people who have an audience, who have educated others on the essential elements of CSS, and who have shared our brand with others.

Most of all, I am grateful for all I have co-created with God in this lifetime!